£5
£c

THE COMPLETE
MACHINE-GUN
1885 to the Present

IAN V. HOGG enlisted in the Royal Artillery during the Second World War and served in Europe and the Far East — including Korea — before becoming an Assistant Instructor in Gunnery at the Royal School of Artillery. In 1966 he joined the staff of the Royal Military College of Science, from which he retired in 1972 with the rank of Master Gunner to become a professional writer.

JOHN BATCHELOR, after serving in the RAF, worked in the technical publications departments of several British aircraft firms before becoming a freelance artist. His work has appeared in a wide range of books and magazines, and his work for Purnell's History of the World War Specials has established him as one of the leading artists in his field.

INTRODUCTION

If any single event can be said to have transformed the history of warfare it was the perfection of the true automatic machine-gun by Hiram Maxim in 1885. Its effect was far greater than the introduction of aircraft or even nuclear weapons to the battlefield. Its importance paralleled the introduction of firearms themselves into a world of arrows and spears.

The appearance of automatic weapons changed not only the face of war but the nations that waged war. The mass destructive power of Vickers, Hotchkiss and Maxim '08 stopped the armies of the old Europe in their tracks and led directly to four years of trenches, gas, the invention of the tank and total war in 1914—18.

However, while the ingenuity of weapons designers took the machine-gun into the air and made it ever more lethally efficient, a new weapon was waiting to give back to the infantryman the offensive power he had lost in the trenches. The submachine-gun appeared in 1918. Some reached the German front-line right at the end of the War but General John T. Thompson's 'trench-broom' was too late and made its name in the gang warfare of Prohibition America.

The Second World War was a war of movement and while the emplaced machine-gun remained the essence of infantry firepower, the submachine-gun was the ideal weapon for the new mechanised soldier. The German armies of the *Blitzkrieg* era were lavishly provided with the MP-38. The British and Americans fought back with Thompson, Sten and M1 and the Russians carried their PPsh-41s all the way to Berlin.

This book is a lavishly illustrated history of the fascinating story of automatic weapons, so important a component of modern warfare. With many full colour illustrations and over a hundred photographs from archives all over the world this book is both a vital reference work and an exciting story of ingenuity and action.

Covered by a .50-in Browning heavy machine-gun, an Israeli patrol sets off along a trench in the Sinai desert. The patrol commander is armed with an Uzi submachine-gun while the other soldiers carry FN rifles

3

CONTENTS

A British corporal in the rubble of Cassino lets loose a hail of fire from his Thompson M1

Imperial War Museum

MECHANICAL MACHINE-GUNS: THE REVOLUTION STARTS

The Defence
James Puckle's gun, patented in 1718, was in effect a flintlock revolver. The chamber in the cylinder was aligned with the barrel by hand, and a crank used to screw it tight and trip the flintlock. It was allegedly intended to fire round balls at Christians and square balls at Turks

Like many other firearms inventions, the success of the machine-gun revolved around the ammunition it fired; while the standard round of ammunition was a lead ball, a heap of gunpowder and a sharpened flint, little in the way of mechanical ingenuity might be expected. But in fact one of the first guns to approach the machine-gun in appearance and design, as well as intent, appeared in the flintlock era.

This was 'The Defence', patented by James Puckle in 1718, a single-barrelled gun with a revolver chamber behind it and a flintlock ignition unit on top of the cylinder. A crank at the rear acted as a screw-jack to force the cylinder against the rear end of the barrel. Once screwed tight, the flintlock was tripped, firing the charge in the chamber and discharging a bullet from the barrel. The operator now swung the crank to unlock the chamber, moved it round to line up the next loaded chamber with the barrel, clamped up and fired again. Once the cylinder was empty – it had six or more chambers – loosening the crank allowed it to be taken off and a fresh one loaded on.

Puckle demonstrated his gun to the Honourable Board of Ordnance in 1717, but they were not impressed and took no further action. He demonstrated it several times; on one occasion in 1722 it fired 63 shots in seven minutes, which was most impressive for the time. But in spite of offering it for sale in a variety of sizes, Puckle never prospered with it. The Duke of Montagu purchased two, using them to arm his expedition to colonise the West Indies, but these appear not to have been used and there is no other record of their purchase and none whatever of their employment. One of the few existing specimens of Puckle's gun is now in the Tower of London.

The next attempts at rapid fire came with the arrival of the percussion cap as a means of ignition. Since placing a cap on the nipple of a firearm was difficult to manage by a mechanical device, the custom arose of piling a number of rifle barrels into some sort of framework and then firing them in succession. This produced a fearsome blast of gunfire for a few seconds, but there was then a long pause while the gunner reloaded all the barrels – all of them muzzle-loaders.

The American Civil War acted as a spur to inventors in this field, and one of the first weapons to approach the mechanical definition of a machine-gun was the 'Agar Coffee Mill Gun' which got its nickname from the appearance of the magazine and operating crank. The gun carried a hopper on top, into which steel tubes containing a lead ball, a charge of powder, and a percussion cap already in place, were dropped. Beneath this was a crank, and turning this pushed a tube into the barrel chamber, locked it there and then dropped a hammer onto the cap. The gun fired, and continued rotation of the crank extracted the tube and ejected it, then began feeding in another. The gunner's mate had his work cut out, picking up the ejected tubes, opening them up and re-loading them, then dropping them into the hopper so as to keep up the fire.

The Agar gun worked, and, for its day, worked well. The trouble was that few people were convinced of it. Those with some smattering of mechanical or scientific knowledge avowed that it was quite ridiculous, though according to Agar it should be possible to fire 100 rounds a minute if the ammunition was prepared. 'Nonsense' said the experts. 'This means you are proposing to explode a pound or so of gunpowder inside the barrel every minute. Steel will never stand up to the heating effect.' There was a good deal of truth in this, of course, but the point would have been better made had they sat down and proposed some system of solving the problem rather than just laughing it to scorn. They had, in fact, put their finger on one of the greatest problems facing the machine-gun designer, but they preferred to ignore it rather than solve it. Poor Agar, in spite of having a war on his doorstep, never sold more than about 50 guns.

Next on the scene was Dr Joseph Requa, who invented a 'Battery Gun' and had it made by one W Billinghurst of Rochester, New York. Hence it became known as the 'Billinghurst-Requa Gun' and consisted of 24 rifle barrels mounted on a wheeled carriage. The gun was demonstrated in New York shortly before the Civil War broke out, and several were purchased by both the Union and Confederate sides. They were often referred to as 'bridge guns' since they were ideal for defending a bridge by delivering a sudden blast of fire into an attacking party.

Requa had got over the problem of the long pause for reloading by making his weapon a breech-loader; indeed, he had almost gone back to Puckle's system. In the Requa gun a number of cartridges were fitted into a sheet-iron frame and dropped in place so that they mated with the breeches of the barrels. Two levers clamped the frame in place and a single percussion cap in the centre of the frame was then fired. The flame from this ignited the nearest cartridges and they, in turn, communicated flame to the remainder, so that the gun fired in a ragged volley.

In August 1863 this weapon was reported on to the Ordnance Select Committee in London. From their report it seems that the whole weapon weighed just over half a ton, was of ·60-in calibre and fired a 414-grain lead ball. But the Committee were not impressed, as their reports shows:

'The Committee are of the opinion that none of the rifle batteries could ever be effectually substituted for field guns of any description, and that even as a device for multiplying and accelerating infantry fire from rifle barrels in the field their utility would be very questionable. The Committee see no occasion for having a gun of this nature specially prepared for trial in this country. Should it be hereafter decided to employ them . . . such instruments could be readily devised by our own mechanicians, without applying to the United States for them.'

Short as it is, this extract from the report pinpoints the greatest problem facing the early development of machine-guns: how were they to be used? It seemed apparent to everybody at the time that they were some sort of artillery weapon, and that they should be handled in the field in the same way, setting down some distance from the enemy and leisurely taking him under fire. It was this question of method of employment which was to be the greatest brake on the early development.

During the time that these guns were being considered in the USA, a European designer had been busy with his version of a battery gun. In 1851 a Belgian inventor, Captain Fafchamps, had designed a weapon which, in some respects, paralleled the Agar gun. He passed his drawings and ideas to a manufacturer named Montigny, who put them into effect and produced the weapon, which was known in consequence as the 'Montigny Mitrailleuse'.

After spending several years on its development and perfection, Montigny managed to interest Napoleon III and in 1869, in great secrecy, the French Army was outfitted with 156 of these guns. They were manufactured in the Meudon Arsenal, only those officers who were to be concerned in operating the weapons being allowed to see them. But in spite of this attempt at secrecy there were a number of 'leaks' to the press, and the newspapers lost no chance of telling the world what a revolutionary weapon the French now had, a miracle gun which would defeat the Prussians with no effort on the French part. Consequently the Prussians were not surprised when they were confronted with them in the war of 1870.

The Mitrailleuse consisted of 25 rifle barrels mounted inside a casing so that, externally, the gun resembled a field gun mounted on the usual sort of two-wheeled carriage. A breech block, fitted with a firing mechanism operating 25 separate firing pins, slid backwards and forwards in the

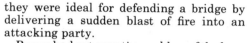

Agar Coffee Mill
Patented in Britain before the American Civil War, Agar's gun used a hopper to deliver loaded steel tubes to the barrel chamber. Operation of the crank locked the tube, tripped a hammer on to the percussion cap, and extracted the empty tube after firing. Although it was possible to fire 100 ·58 in balls per minute, military conservatism prevented it being adopted in any quantity

Billinghurst-Requa Battery Gun
Twenty-four rifle barrels mounted on a wheeled carriage were loaded with ·60-in cartridges in an iron frame. Ignition of a single percussion cap produced a ragged volley, but lack of imagination again prevented its adoption

barrel casing when a loading lever was operated by hand. The cartridges were carried in a metal plate which had 25 holes drilled in it corresponding to the arrangement of the barrels. With the breech block slid backwards, this plate, loaded with cartridges, was dropped into grooves on the forward face of the block. The block was then pushed forward, whereupon the cartridges entered the chambers of their respective barrels and the firing mechanism was cocked. Revolving a crank at the rear of the gun now caused the firing pins to fall in succession, faster or slower according to the speed at which the crank was turned. Normal rate of fire was a quick spin of the crank which fired all 25 barrels in one second. With a supply of ready-loaded plates handy a three-man crew could keep up a rate of about 250 rounds per minute.

In addition to the Mitrailleuses, the French had bought a number of Gatling guns (of which we shall see more), and they went to war in 1870 in high spirits. But the war was an unmitigated disaster, for many reasons, and one of the least successful areas was the records of the machine-guns. The faults lay not with the mechanism of the guns but with their tactical handling; there was still doubt about whether they were infantry weapons or artillery weapons, and since they looked like artillery they were handled the same way, being brought into action wheel to wheel in open positions. Since the maximum range of the Mitrailleuse was about 1800 yards, and the maximum range of the Prussian artillery about 2500 yards, the result was a foregone conclusion. As soon as the French unlimbered their machine-guns the Prussian artillery opened up and pounded them into impotence.

It could have been the death-knell of the machine-gun, but fortunately the fault was recognised as one of employment and not of operation, and the guns survived – just.

The Austrians had been sufficiently impressed by the mechanical ability of the Mitrailleuse to purchase another design of Montigny gun, with 37 barrels chambered for the 11-mm Werndl cartridge. But instead of using them as field weapons they reserved them for fortification defence, a role that most military authorities agreed was ideal for such weapons. The guns would be within a protected fort where they could be served and reloaded in safety, while the volume of fire was just what was needed to deal with sudden assaults against the ramparts.

But the Mitrailleuse was overshadowed by its American contemporary, the Gatling gun, one of the most famous of all machine-guns and certainly the best-known of the mechanical weapons if not the most perfect. The Gatling was invented in 1861 by Dr Richard Jordan Gatling; although qualified in medicine he never practised, and spent most of his life inventing, though of all his inventions only the gun has survived to perpetuate his name, his steam-plough, hemp-breaker and rice-planter having faded from view.

Gatling more or less took the Agar system of loading a cartridge by a forward stroke of a crank and applied it to the metallic cartridge. He also appreciated the

Montigny Mitrailleuse Cartridge

point about the heating effect of firing pounds of gunpowder in a barrel, and arranged his gun to have six barrels which would be fired in turn. Thus if the gun had a rate of fire of, say, 600 rounds per minute, any one barrel would only be firing at 100 rpm, and it would have an opportunity to cool down during the time that the other five were being fired. The six barrels were mounted around a central axis, and behind them was the loading and firing arrangement operated by a crank at the side of the gun. The cartridges were placed into a feeding box on top of the gun and fell into the mechanism by gravity.

When the crank was turned the six barrels and the breech mechanism revolved around the axis; each barrel had a bolt and firing pin controlled by a cam groove in the breech casing. As the unit revolved, projections in the bolts, riding in the groove, caused the bolts to open and close in the barrel breeches. Taking one barrel as an example, at the topmost position in its revolution the breech was open and a cartridge from the feed column fell in. As the barrel continued to move round, the bolt was closed by the cam groove and the cartridge was forced into the gun chamber. The bolt was then locked and as the barrel reached the bottom-most position the cam tripped the firing pin and the cartridge was fired. Then as the barrel began to move up the other side of the circle the bolt was

Montigny Mitrailleuse (Witte Interpretation)

In January 1865 his perfected model was tested by the US War Department, and in the following year it was officially adopted, 50 guns of 1-in calibre and 50 of ·50-in being ordered. With this to sustain him, Gatling began to sell the gun throughout the world.

The British Army began to take an interest in the Gatling in 1869, and in 1870 a most comprehensive trial was carried out, in which the Gatling was compared with the Montigny Mitrailleuse, a 12-pounder breech-loader firing shrapnel, a 9-pounder muzzle-loader firing shrapnel, six soldiers firing Martini-Henry rifles and six soldiers firing Snider rifles. The Gatling fired 492 lb of ammunition and obtained 2803 hits on various targets; the Montigny fired 472 lb for 1708 hits; the 12-pounder 1232 lb for 2286 hits; and the 9-pounder 1013 lb for 2207 hits. This certainly proved the economy of the Gatling gun.

In a test of timed fire, the Gatling fired 1925 rounds in 2·5 minutes to score 651 hits; the Montigny, in the same time, 1073 rounds to obtain 214 hits; the six men firing Martini-Henry rifles got off 391 rounds for 152 hits, and the six with Snider rifles 313 rounds for 82 hits. This trial was fired at various ranges, and the Gatling stood out for its accuracy at 900 yards, managing a far higher percentage of hits at long range than did any of the other competitors.

Immediate introduction

The Ordnance Select Committee said in their report that 'of the two systems of machine-guns . . . the Gatling has proved to be far superior . . .' and went on to recommend 'The immediate introduction of the small Gatling gun for employment in the field . . . for a first instalment, 50 guns of the small calibre (0·42-in) for land service, and as many of the small and medium sized (0·65-in) guns as the Lords Commissioners may consider requisite for the Navy, to be ordered from Dr Gatling, pending the preparation of suitable plant either at Enfield or Woolwich for future production'.

At more or less the same time the Russian government, looking to the prospect of a war with Turkey, ordered 400 Gatling guns. Their General Gorloff was sent to America to superintend the preparation of these weapons and he, with considerable astuteness, had nameplates bearing his own name manufactured and fixed to the guns before they went to Russia. They were thereafter known as 'Gorloff' guns, and an article in the *Journal de St Petersburg* of 27 November 1870 is not without interest as an example of early Russian propaganda:

'The mitrailleuse adopted in Russia is on a model invented by Major-General Gorloff and based upon the American Gatling system. The Gorloff gun, however, only resembles the Gatling in exterior form and is quite original. In perfecting his arm, Dr Gatling has, it appears, been guilty of important plagiarisms on the Gorloff model, which has a just title to the name of the "Russian mitrailleuse".' So as well as the wheel, sliced bread and sex, it seems that the Russians also invented the Gatling gun.

Be that as it may, the Russians used the Gatling/Gorloff to good effect when they finally went to war with the Turks in 1877. The siege of Plevna gave opportunity for testing it in positional warfare, while some of the operations in Central Asia showed how effective it could be in dealing with cavalry charges.

The British took a number of Gatlings to

Montigny Mitrailleuse

The original Mitrailleuse (or 'grape shot shooter') had 37 barrels, and was the invention of the Belgian Captain Fafchamps. The mechanism of the gun (below) used a lever to push the breech forward, locking a ready-loaded plate in place. The firing pins were operated by a crank at the side, a quick spin firing all the barrels in about a second, and about 12 plates (444 rounds) could be fired per minute. Redesigned by Commandant de Reffye with 25 barrels, it was issued to the French army in time for the Franco-Prussian War of 1870. Unfortunately, it was used as a field gun, with disastrous results.

unlocked and opened, the cartridge case extracted and ejected, and it arrived once more at the top, empty, ready to be reloaded.

It should perhaps be said that the description above is of the perfected Gatling; the first models, understandably, were not quite so neat and tidy, although they were quite serviceable. General Ben Butler thought sufficient of them to buy 12 (at $1000 apiece), which he used successfully at Petersburg, Virginia, but apart from that Gatling made little headway during the Civil War; it seems that his sympathies were suspected by both sides.

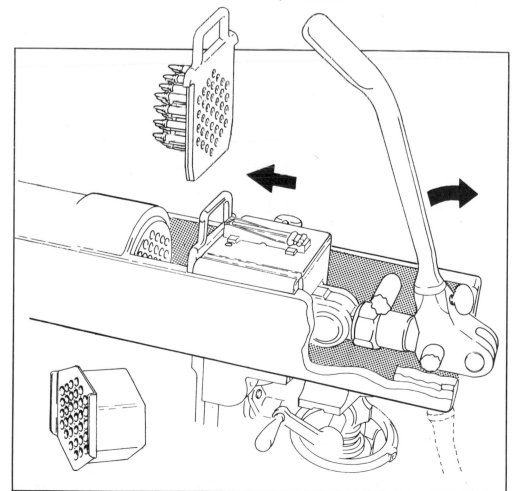

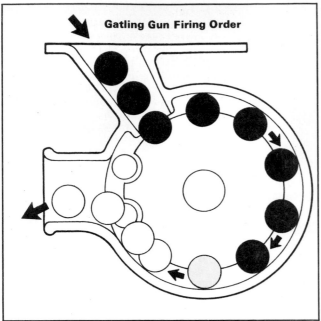

Gatling Gun Firing Order

the Zulu War in 1879. Captain Campbell of HMS *Active*, who commanded the Naval Brigade, reported: 'About 300 rounds were fired from the *Active's* Gatling gun at the battle of Inyezane, the effect was to immediately dislodge a number of Zulus from the bush at which the fire was directed; throughout the campaign the gun worked most satisfactorily. . . .'

In 1883 the gun was greatly improved by the adoption of a drum feed system developed by James G Accles, an Australian engineer who was, at the time, project engineer for Gatling. Accles, it should be said, later went to England where he was associated with the Gatling Arms and Ammunition Company of Birmingham, a company having no connection with Gatling except to act as agents for the sale of his guns in Europe. While with this company, Accles developed an improved model of the Gatling which was sold in small numbers as the 'Accles Positive Feed Machine-Gun'.

The drum feed system certainly improved the reliability of the weapon and also allowed rates of fire of up to 1200 rpm to be reached with the hand-cranked gun. Since this feed system seemed capable of even higher rates, in 1893 Gatling produced a gun which used an electric motor to rotate the barrels, and with this he achieved the phenomenal rate of 3000 rpm. However, nobody seemed very interested in this, since by that time automatic machine-guns which needed no outside power supply – man or motor – had appeared, and the day of the mechanical machine-gun was drawing to its close.

In an attempt to convert the Gatling into an automatic gun, in 1895 Dr Gatling produced his last modification in which part of the gas behind the bullet was tapped off and used to operate a lever which turned the barrel group. While it worked, it was far from being as mechanically perfect as the competing automatic guns and very few examples of the gas-operated Gatling were ever made.

Dr Gatling died in 1903 and his gun survived him by some years, remaining in US service until 1911; the Gatling guns in British service had been declared obsolete on 24 March 1905. It appears that the last time Gatlings were used in combat was during the siege of Port Arthur in the Russo-Japanese War, when several Gorloff guns

formed part of the armament of the forts surrounding Port Arthur.

During the life of the Gatling gun, other inventors had not been idle. One of the first to appear was William Gardner of Ohio, who sold his patents to a newly-formed engineering company called Pratt & Whitney. Pratt had been an engineer with Colt's Patent Firearms Company and so he had some appreciation of what was involved in the design and manufacture of firearms. Between them, he and Gardner developed one of the best of the mechanical machine-guns.

It consisted of two barrels mounted side by side, the bolts being operated by two cranks on a cross-axle driven by an outside handle. Basically, the mechanism was like a two-cylinder motor laid on its side, the pistons being the breech-bolts. Feed was

Gardner Machine-gun
Invented by William Gardner, and built by the fledgling Pratt & Whitney company, this twin-barrelled gun worked extremely well. It was capable of roughly 365 rpm, and was used widely by shore parties of the Royal Navy after its adoption in 1884

from a vertical magazine which held the cartridges by their rims. As the rounds fell into the gun, so a feed arm moved across and dropped them into the breech of the appropriate barrel. As the crank revolved, so the breeches opened and closed alternately; as one gun fired the other was empty, and as one bolt closed the other opened.

The Gardner was an extremely safe and reliable design; on its trials in 1879 it astonished the observers by firing 10,000 rounds in 27 minutes 36 seconds, a rate of about 365 rpm, which was no mean achievement for a hand-operated gun. But in spite of this the US authorities showed no interest; they had the Gatling and that was all they wanted. So Gardner went to Britain and demonstrated his guns there.

Strangely enough, the first gun he demonstrated was a single-barrelled model, an uncommon version of his design, in December 1880. Gardner fired 500 rounds in 3 minutes 12 seconds without any failures; the gun was then dropped into a tank of cold water to cool it, hauled out and firing was immediately resumed without even stopping to wipe the water off the gun. It

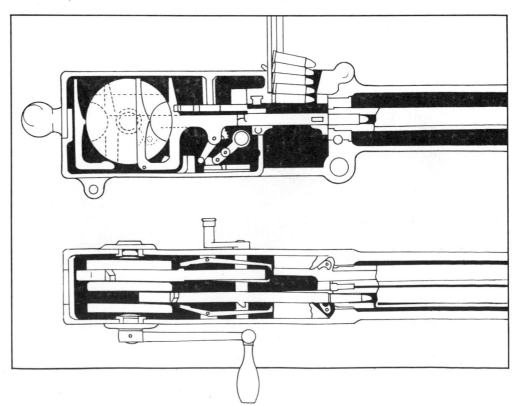

Gatling Gun
The first Gatling gun, built in 1860, was
a six-barrelled hopper-fed weapon. Subsequent
improvements were incorporated in the ·65-in
drum-fed model shown here, built by Colt
after the Civil War and tested by the British
Army in 1870. (Details for this illustration
taken from Army Code Book 60525,
Handbook of Land Service Ammunition Part 1)

Gatling-equipped Camel
A trooper of the Afghan Camel Corps in
1874–77. Gatling's 'Camel Gun' was built in
prototype in 1871 and manufactured in 1874.
Using a ·45-in cartridge and weighing 135 lb
it was designed to be fired from a tripod
or from the back of a camel or elephant

continued to function perfectly, and without
further argument the committee assembled
to test the weapon recommended the purchase of 20 guns. Gardner later went on
to demonstrate his multi-barrelled guns
and these too were accepted for service in
their turn.

The other machine-gun adopted by Britain
in considerable numbers was the Nordenfelt,
the invention of a Swedish engineer, Helge
Palmkranz. In order to finance his invention,
Palmkranz approached a Swedish banker,
Torsten Nordenfelt, and thereafter the invention was known as the Nordenfelt gun.
Perhaps he deserved the fame, for he
certainly worked hard at publicising his
gun, never failing to show up whenever
there was an opportunity of demonstrating
it to anyone who might be interested.

In 1880 a four-barrelled gun in 1-in calibre
was adopted by the British Navy and shortly
thereafter several other navies followed suit.
This was the time of the torpedo boats –
small, fast ships, armed with torpedoes,
which could rush up to a ponderous battle-
ship or into a harbour, loose off two or
three torpedoes, turn away and make off
at high speed. The slow-moving armament of
the big guns could not hope to catch these
gadflies, and a heavy calibre fast-firing
machine-gun seemed to have the best chance
of stopping them. As a result the Nordenfelt
prospered.

The Nordenfelt was another multi-barrelled gun, the number of barrels ranging
from two to ten or even twelve, and operation was by a handle on the right of the gun
which was pushed back and forth. On the
forward stroke a carrier block, which
carried the cartridges delivered from an
overhead hopper, was moved into line with
the barrels. A breech block then moved
forward to chamber the rounds and an action
block, containing the firing pins, moved in
behind the breech block and lined up with

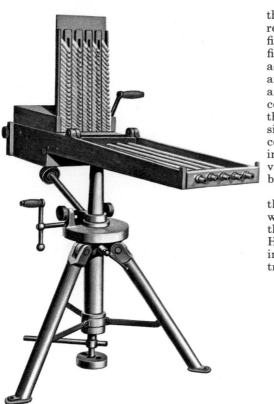

the caps of the cartridges. As the handle reached the end of its forward stroke the firing pins were tripped and the barrels fired. On the return stroke of the lever the action block moved away, the breech opened and extracted the empty cartridge cases, and the carrier block moved into place to collect a fresh loading of cartridges from the hopper. The whole action was very simple, very robust and very reliable and it could handle virtually any size of cartridge in complete safety. The Nordenfelt, in various configurations of two, four and ten barrels, remained in service until 1903.

Nordenfelt's principal competitor was the Hotchkiss Revolver Cannon, another weapon devised with the torpedo boat threat in mind. Benjamin Berkeley Hotchkiss, born in Watertown, Connecticut in 1826, had spent most of his life in the gun trade and had tried to market a multi-

Nordenfelt Machine-gun
Designed by a Swede, Helge Palmkranz, and marketed by the famous armaments tycoon Torsten Nordenfelt, this was a simple, robust and reliable gun. Made with two to ten barrels in calibres up to 37-mm, the five-barrelled, ·45-in Royal Navy version is illustrated

Gatling Bulldog
The smallest of all Gatling guns was patented in July 1893. Intended for use by police, and shown here with a member of the New York Police Department, its six barrels were only 12 in long. Encased in bronze, it had a new extraction system designed to minimise the jamming that was characteristic of Gatling guns

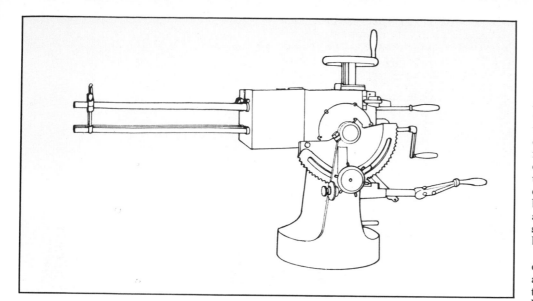

Fitzgerald Battery Gun
Even after the advent of the automatic machine-gun, inventors continued to produce mechanical weapons. The Fitzgerald gun was demonstrated to the Royal Navy in 1907: predictably, it was turned down

Hotchkiss Revolver Cannon
Patented by Benjamin Hotchkiss in Paris in 1894, this 37-mm cannon fired a 1-lb shell and was intended as an anti-torpedo boat weapon. Over 10,000 were built, and it was used by the French, Belgian, British, Dutch, Italian, Russian and US navies

barrelled gun. Seeing that the Nordenfelt had the edge on his design, he turned to a fresh look at the Gatling system.

In 1874, while living in Paris, he patented his revolver gun which, as the name implies, was a battery of five barrels revolving around a central axis very much like the Gatling. However, although its appearance was like that of the Gatling, its action was considerably different, the barrels not moving continuously but being indexed around one fifth of a full turn with pauses to allow the various operations of loading, firing and extraction to be carried out with the barrels still. Belt-fed, the gun was designed around a one-pound, 37-mm calibre shell, since its principal use was intended to be bombarding torpedo boats.

Numbers of Hotchkiss cannon were purchased by various navies, and the French also bought them to protect harbour entrances. Hotchkiss died in Paris in 1885 but his company continued in the gunmaking business and was later to develop and produce one of the most widely-distributed machine-guns in the world.

Misguided inventors

By the time of Hotchkiss's death the automatic machine-gun had appeared and the mechanical machine-gun was beginning to be relegated to second place. Even so, there was no shortage of inventors who were so convinced of the perfection of their inventions that they persisted in trying to interest the world's armies in mechanical machine-guns right into the twentieth century. It will serve no useful purpose to tabulate all these misguided gentlemen, but it is worth noting that a mechanical battery gun, the Fitzgerald, was demonstrated to the Royal Navy as late as 1907 – without success, it may be added.

Most of the mechanical guns used conventional ammunition, but there is one variety which deserves mention because it proposed to do away with cartridges entirely, launching the bullets purely by mechanical means. This was the centrifugal gun, an idea which recurs in the patent files from time to time and is probably not dead yet.

The basic idea is to spin a disc very rapidly, and then drop balls on to it. The spinning action forces the balls outwards, imparting velocity to them, until they arrive at the edge of the disc and are flung off at high speed. By suitable design it is possible to give direction to the balls so that there is a constant stream of projectiles being discharged in the desired direction.

In theory it sounds very attractive, but in practice it never works – the laws of conservation of energy see to that. Nevertheless, it has occupied the time of innumerable inventors over the years. It appeared several times in the nineteenth century, was put forward to the British Army in 1915 by no less a personage than Major-General Baden-Powell, the hero of Mafeking, and, to the author's knowledge, appeared for the last time in Italy in 1944, the invention of a pair of ingenious Italian soldiers.

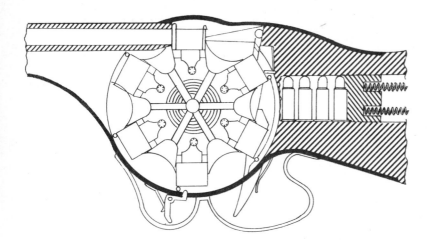

Clair Circular Magazine Gun
The French Clair Brothers were among the earliest to patent automatic weapons — some of which actually worked. One of their less probable ideas is this rotary machine-gun of 1893. The drawing actually shows their gas-operated system applied to a pistol but they claimed it could also be adopted in machine-guns. It never was

Enterprise and Ingenuity

There has never been any shortage of inventors willing to try their hands at designing machine-guns, and especially during the late 19th century, when the weapon was something of a novelty. On these pages we show drawings taken from the official British patents books of the late 19th and early 20th centuries covering Abridgement Class Ordnance

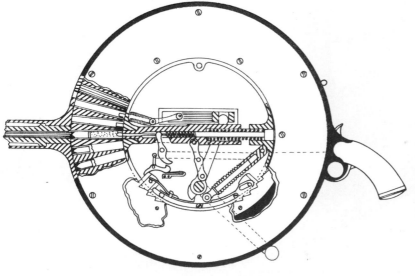

Perry Rotary Machine-gun
This is the invention of Asa Byron, Benjamin Franklin and Fidelia Lillie, brothers and sisters of the Perry family of Grand Junction, Colorado. Patented in 1903, it covers a clockwork-driven machine-gun or rifle. Cartridges were fed from a magazine in the butt to a clockwork-driven rotary feeder which carried the rounds to the breech and held them there while fired. After firing, the wheel turns forward so that the carrier is sprung apart by the barrel and the empty case falls out. Although well thought out, it is unlikely ever to have worked

Armanni Machine-gun
Mr Armanni took out a patent in 1886 for this highly unlikely machine-gun. It operates on blowback principles and the magazine rotates so as to bring a fresh chamber and cartridge in front of the bolt every time the gun fires. Perhaps the most entertaining feature is the little brush which cleans out the chamber after each shot

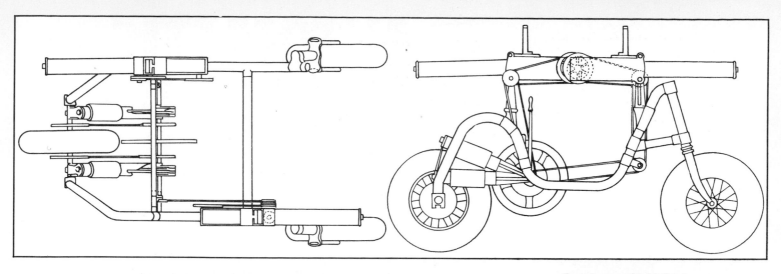

Pennington Field Cycle

One of the first applications of the motor vehicle to the machine-gun was this invention of E J Pennington in 1896. The tricycle is powered by two 'oil motors' which also, through a series of chains, drive the machine-guns, one of which points in each direction. Notice that the pneumatic tyre is featured, but Pennington seems not to have heard of the automatic machine-gun yet and was still thinking in terms of mechanical weapons

Apostoloff Horse Carriage

A 1904 patent by S B Apostoloff which might well be called putting the cart before the horse. One feels that the operator would have had his work cut out to control and steer the machine without the added complication of firing the machine-gun

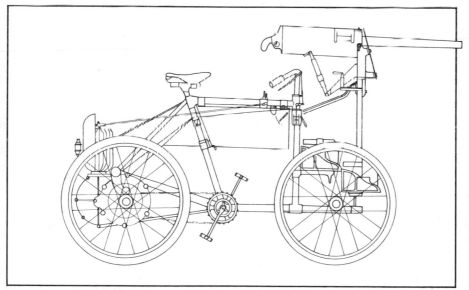

Simms Quadricycle

F R Simms is among the few inventors of self-propelled machine-guns who managed to see his inventions in the flesh. This 1899 patent covers his 'quadricycle' with a Maxim gun at the front and a petrol engine at the back. The gun could be dismounted or fired from the quadricycle. Under the title of the 'Simms Motor Scout' it was demonstrated widely in 1900

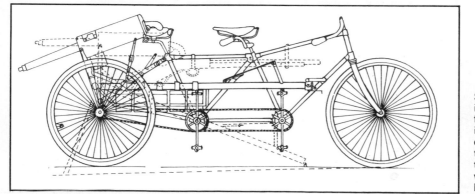

Maxim & Silverman Tandem Cycle

Sir Hiram Maxim did not rest content with inventing the machine-gun but also put forward some novel ideas on how to use it in the field. Here is his 1895 design for carrying two guns on the back of a tandem. Steadying bars could be lowered to support the machine when stopped while the two riders jumped off and began firing the guns

The mechanical machine-guns all relied on the input of some sort of effort from outside in order to operate their machinery, usually a man operating a crank or lever of some sort. This seemed quite satisfactory at the time, since the only sources of power other than men were far too complicated or cumbersome to be carried onto the battlefield and set to work to drive a machine-gun. And things might have stayed that way for a long time had it not been for the inquiring mind of one man – Hiram Stevens Maxim.

Inventive genius

Hiram Maxim was born in Sangerville, Maine, in 1840 and was apprenticed to a coachbuilder. After this he worked in a machine shop and in a shipbuilding yard. He had a wide-ranging inventive faculty which embraced such things as electric lights, gas generating plants, steam and vacuum pumps, engine governors and even a steam-driven aeroplane.

In 1881 he attended the Electrical Exhibition in Paris and, so the story goes, was told by an acquaintance that his sure way to financial success was to 'invent something that will enable these fool Europeans to kill each other quicker'. Whether this tale is true or not, Maxim went to London and set up a small workshop in Hatton Garden where he began to examine the contemporary state of the machine-gun. He soon put his finger on the vital point – when a gun was fired a vast amount of energy was liberated, only a small portion of which was used in propelling the bullet. The rest was going to waste, and Maxim resolved to try and adapt this wasted energy to the task of operating the various functions of the gun.

AUTOMATIC MACHINE-GUNS: FOR MAXIMUM KILLING POWER

Between 1882 and 1885 he analysed every possible way of using this energy, devised ways of applying the energy to the gun, and patented every conceivable way of operating a gun. Indeed, had Maxim been sufficiently hostile he could probably, on the strength of his many patents, have stifled every other machine-gun at birth for the next quarter-century, since almost every successful design carries traces of a Maxim patent in it.

He eventually concluded that the most reliable system of operation would be to harness the recoil force of the weapon, and in 1885 he demonstrated his 'first' model, the first successful automatic machine-gun. It was chambered for the British service ·45-in Martini-Henry cartridge, and its method of operation was considerably different from anything which had been seen before. (It should also be said that it was considerably different from the system he eventually perfected for the machine-

guns which were to become famous under his name.)

When the gun was ready to fire, with a cartridge in the chamber, the barrel and breech block were securely locked together by a large hook engaging in the block. When fired, the two units recoiled together for about half an inch, whereupon the hook was lifted and the barrel stopped. The breech block was then free to continue recoiling, extracting and ejecting the spent case as it travelled back. The block was attached to a connecting rod and crank, and the recoil stroke caused the crank to revolve through three-quarters of a turn. As it reached the rear dead centre position the striker was cocked, and the momentum of the crank carried it past this dead point, reversing the movement of the block so as to load a fresh round and close the breech.

The next shot fired would rotate the crank in the opposite direction until it

Hiram Maxim (inset), inventor of the automatic machine-gun, with the improved 1885 version of his original gun. Below: German troops in 1914 with their heavy, sledge-mounted 7·92-mm Maxim Model 1908

stopped, with the breech closed once more, in the position from which it had begun the recoil for the previous round. Maxim adopted this system of partial rotation in opposite directions in order to avoid the danger of the acceleration of the crank causing the gun to run away with itself, firing faster and faster until something gave way.

Ammunition was delivered by a belt to a 12-chambered rotary feed block, from which the rounds were fed to the breech. The final refinement was a hydraulic buffer mechanism connected to the crank. This not only absorbed various mechanical stresses but was also adapted to act as a rate-of-fire controller. Adjusting the hydraulic valve regulated the movement of the crank, and the gun could be set to fire at any desired rate from 1 to 600 rpm.

Maxim demonstrated this gun in front of the Duke of Cambridge and other military notables and aroused a certain amount of interest, but they were non-committal. So his next step was to re-examine the weapon and redesign it, making it simpler, lighter and more reliable.

The new model was completed in 1885. This still used recoil as the driving force but did away with the cumbersome locking hook, replacing it with a toggle joint. An extension frame attached to the barrel carried the 'lock' – or breech block – which was kept firmly closed by a toggle joint anchored to a cross-shaft at the rear of the extension.

The action of the toggle joint can best be imagined by thinking of the human leg, which it closely resembles. Both the leg and the toggle unit consist of two solid sections – the shin and the thigh – connected by a joint – the knee. Imagine the leg as the toggle in the Maxim gun. The hip is the joint at the end of the barrel extension, while the sole of the foot is the breech block. If the toggle – or leg – is extended in a straight line, any pressure on the foot – such as the explosion of the cartridge – will pass straight up the leg and be resisted by the anchorage of the hip bone to the barrel extension. But if someone were to tap the underside of the knee joint, then there would no longer be any resistance and the leg would fold up; in other words, the toggle would fold and the breech block would be able to move away from the barrel.

In Maxim's toggle joint the operation was downward. As the whole unit, barrel, barrel extension and toggle, recoiled to the rear, the barrel and breech block were securely locked together so that the full force of the exploding cartridge was driving the bullet from the gun and there was no danger of the breech opening while the chamber pressure was high. After about half an inch of movement a crank handle on the end of the cross-shaft struck a fixed roller, and this gave the toggle a downward impulse which broke the joint and accelerated the breech block backwards while the barrel remained still. At the same time rotation of the shaft wound a spring.

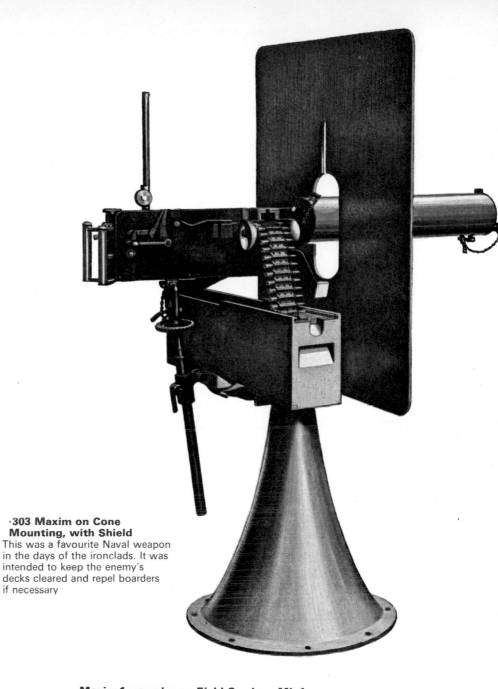

·303 Maxim on Cone Mounting, with Shield
This was a favourite Naval weapon in the days of the ironclads. It was intended to keep the enemy's decks cleared and repel boarders if necessary

Maxim 1-pounder on Field Carriage Mk 1
This was introduced in 1900 for service in South Africa, issued with the intention of countering the 1-pounder Maxim 'Pom Pom' guns in Boer hands. After the war these carriages were modified to become the Army's first anti-aircraft mountings

Russian machine-gun crews tow their Model 1910 Maxims into captivity

When the toggle came to a halt, this spring reversed the movement and drove the block forward, loading a fresh round and lifting the toggle once more until it resumed its locked position. With the abandonment of the part-rotational crank system the hydraulic buffer and rate of fire controller was also dropped, and the gun now had only two options – single shots or 600 rpm.

With the design perfected, Maxim toured Europe giving demonstrations and firing in competition with the contemporary mechanical guns – not that there was much of a contest, so convincing was the Maxim gun's performance – and the orders soon began to flow in. The Maxim Gun Company was formed, using manufacturing facilities at the Vickers factory at Crayford in Kent, and guns were supplied to the British, Austrian, German, Swiss, Italian and Russian governments by 1890.

The first combat use of the Maxim was in the newly formed colony of the Gambia, on 21 November 1888. A small punitive expedition under General Sir Francis de Winton was sent out to deal with a tribe who had been raiding various settlements and among the armament was a ·45-in Maxim gun. On arrival at the fortified village of Robari, the General himself set up the Maxim and opened fire. According

Maxim Action
The barrel recoiled on firing, carrying the toggle and breech block with it. The curved crank handle was forced against its stop and made to rotate the crank in a clockwise motion, making the toggle break downwards, allowing the breech to open as the barrel halted. The crank movement tensioned the 'fusee spring' to provide power to close the breech and reload the gun.

to his despatch, 'the bullets rained in through the portholes and between the planks, killing numbers of the enemy. The breastwork and other towers were treated in the same manner, and in a few minutes it was seen that the garrison were issuing from the fort and flying for their lives'.

The success of the Maxim gun soon led other inventors to look at the possibilities of driving an automatic gun by using the gun's own energy. Among the first was another notable American gun designer, John Moses Browning. Browning had already made a name for himself by designing repeating rifles and shotguns, and in 1889 he began working on a machine-gun. While he fully understood Maxim's use of recoil, he was of the opinion that muzzle blast was an even more fruitful source of energy, and his first models were based on the use of a plate to trap the excess gas after the exit of the bullet and, through the medium of levers, operate the breech.

He then drilled a hole in the gun barrel, close to the muzzle, and led the gas into a cylinder. Here it propelled a piston which in turn carried out the various functions of loading, firing and extracting. This was the first true gas-operated gun. By 1890 he had perfected his design and offered it to the Colt company; a prototype model was made and tested by the US Navy in 1892–3, being adopted into service as the Model 1895.

These guns are almost always called the 'Potato Digger' guns due to their unusual action. The gas is tapped off just before the muzzle, but instead of driving a piston in a

cylinder, it drives an arm hinged beneath the barrel. Thus the arm describes an arc, swinging down and back, and thus driving the gun mechanism. While this is an unusual mechanism, it is also a very efficient one in that it delivers the force of the gas very gently, absorbing shock and keeping the rate of fire down to a practical figure.

The principal drawback was that the gun had to be used on a tripod or other high-set mounting: otherwise the swinging arm would dig into the ground. But as the tacticians of the day had not yet got around to thinking about men crawling around the battlefield with machine-guns, there was little notice taken of that side of things.

In Europe, the first local design of an automatic gun came from Austria. In 1888 Archduke Karl Salvator and Count Dormus patented a gun operating on a delayed blowback system. In this system the breech block was never positively locked to the barrel, but was held closed by its own inertia, plus that of a pivoting block and the force of a powerful spring. As a result the bullet was out of the muzzle and the gas pressure had dropped before the breech had begun to open.

Being a mechanically simple design it was quite reliable, but the lack of a positive lock meant that only relatively weak cartridges were safe in the gun. It was adopted by the Austro-Hungarian Army as their Model 1893 and was mostly used in fortifications. A later model, the 1902, improved the system of feed – a gravity-operated overhead box – but few of these

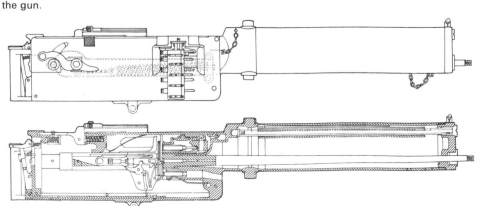

Maxim Model 1910

The Russians bought their first Maxims in the 1890s, and later set up their own factory to make them. This 7·62-mm model, on the Sokolov carriage, was used during two World Wars and by the Chinese in Korea. Its main drawback was its weight, including carriage, of 162·5 lb

seem to have been made. The M1909 was a great improvement, using a belt feed – though it was a pretty peculiar belt – and finally came a 1913 model which tried, once more, to improve the feed system which had always been one of the machine-gun's weak points. It might be noted that this gun was always referred to as the Skoda, after the company that made it; Salvator and von Dormus never achieved any fame from it.

In France the Hotchkiss Company was now directed by another American, Laurence V Benet, and in 1893 he was approached by another Austrian, Captain Adolf Odkolek, with the design of a gas-operated gun. Benet could see that the

Maxim on Pack Saddle

Issued to mountain troopers. The pack also carried the folded tripod and two boxes of ammunition on each side. The whole outfit was fitted with quick-release catches and could be off-loaded and brought into action in a matter of seconds

design had some useful features, though he could also see that it was going to take some hard work before it became a practical gun, and he bought the design and patents from Odkolek for a fixed sum, refusing any sort of royalty deal. This meant that Odkolek lost out on a near-fortune.

In Odkolek's design there was a gas cylinder beneath the barrel in which a piston operated to drive the gun mechanism. The breech was locked by a pivoting

locking flap controlled by the movement of the gas piston, and the ammunition was carried in a pressed metal strip which was entered into the gun on the right hand side. As the bolt operated, so rounds were pulled from the strip and the strip moved across until it fell, empty, from the left side of the gun.

The Hotchkiss was adopted by the French army in 1897; it proved to be moderately reliable but was prone to overheating, in spite of massive brass cooling fins on the barrel. It was succeeded by a Model 1900 in which the barrel had been redesigned with steel cooling fins in the hope of improving matters. This was slightly better.

It was not, however, good enough for the French army and they set themselves the

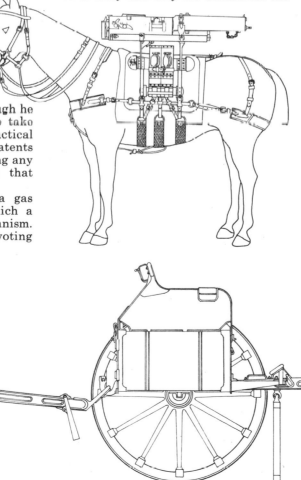

task of redesigning the Hotchkiss, without reference to the Hotchkiss company, with results which were disastrous.

The first attempt was introduced as the 'Puteaux' or Model 1905 gun; it was more or less the 1900 Hotchkiss with a lot more brass fins on the barrel and a variable rate-of-fire device of questionable utility. The gun proved to be a failure and it was withdrawn from line units and put into fortifications as a fixed defence gun.

The next attempt was the 'St Etienne', or Model 1907, which can best be described as a Hotchkiss with everything changed around simply for the sake of changing. It used the same gas piston – but now the piston was blown forward, instead of back, and so there had to be a gear system to reverse the movement and make sure that the breech block went back as the piston went forward. The well-tried Hotchkiss bolt lock was thrown out and a peculiar over-centre unit, resembling a Maxim toggle, was put in. The gas cylinder had an adjustable volume so that the rate of fire could be altered by slowing or speeding up the action of the piston. The return spring was mounted close beneath the barrel, and this, allied with the well-known propensity of the design for overheating, more or less guaranteed that the spring would lose its temper (in the metallurgical sense) before much firing had been done.

In fact the only thing that the designers failed to alter was the strip feed system, which most people agree was the only really faulty feature of the original

·303 Maxim on Carriage

The 'Carriage Machine Gun Cavalry or Mounted Infantry' allowed the Maxim to accompany mounted formations in South Africa. The crew rode on the limber, which also carried ammunition, spare parts, axe, shovel and other

equipment. To go into action the carriage was unhooked and a bicycle saddle clipped to the trail leg to allow the gunner to sit and fire the gun while his assistant knelt alongside and supplied fresh ammunition belts from the limber

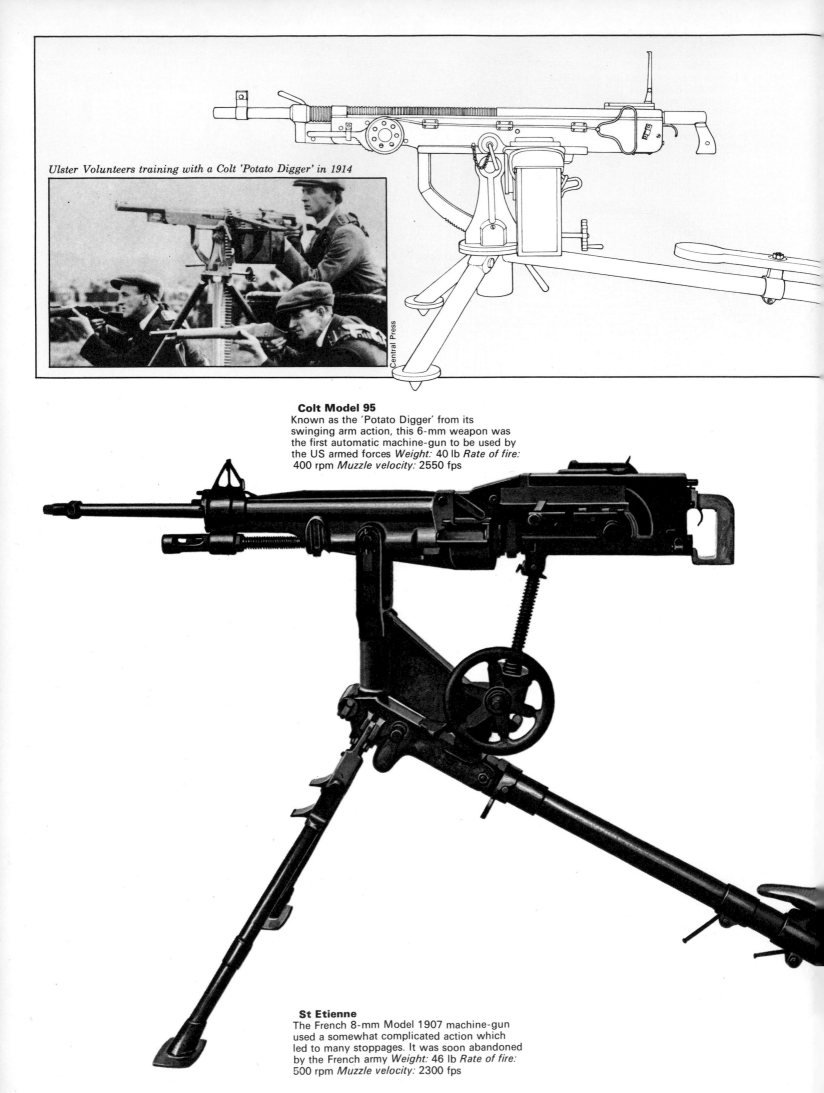

Ulster Volunteers training with a Colt 'Potato Digger' in 1914

Colt Model 95
Known as the 'Potato Digger' from its
swinging arm action, this 6-mm weapon was
the first automatic machine-gun to be used by
the US armed forces *Weight:* 40 lb *Rate of fire:*
400 rpm *Muzzle velocity:* 2550 fps

St Etienne
The French 8-mm Model 1907 machine-gun
used a somewhat complicated action which
led to many stoppages. It was soon abandoned
by the French army *Weight:* 46 lb *Rate of fire:*
500 rpm *Muzzle velocity:* 2300 fps

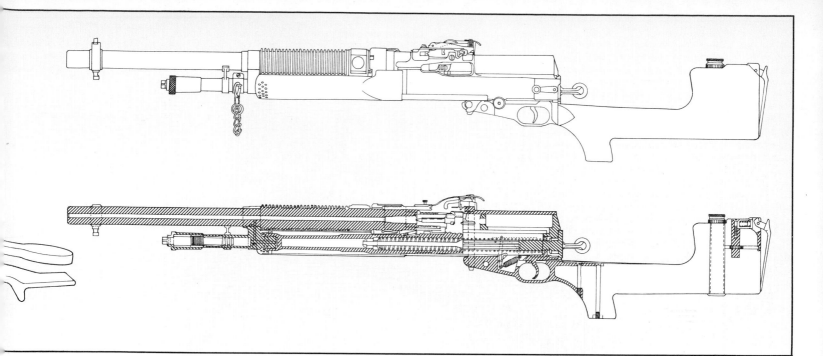

Hotchkiss · 303 Mk 1
This strip-fed light machine-gun was produced
in 1908 and introduced the 'fermeture nut'
method of locking the bolt. Adopted by the
British as the Hotchkiss Machine-gun Mark 1,
Cavalry, by the US as the Benet-Mercie, and
by the French as their Model 1908, it was
never particularly successful, though it
remained in service with the Indian Army until
the early 1930s *Weight:* 27 lb *Rate of fire:*
650 rpm *Muzzle velocity:* 2440 fps

Skoda Model 1909
One of the few delayed blowback guns to
succeed. This model was an improvement on the
original model of 1893, using belt feed and an
optical sighting system, but the mechanism
demanded lubricated cartridges. It was used
throughout the First World War

Hotchkiss design. After numbers of these guns had been built the First World War broke out and soon exposed them for the hopeless mechanical oddities that they were. The French army were then very glad to get back to the original Hotchkiss and sent the St Etienne guns off to the Foreign Legion as quickly as possible.

The Hotchkiss was bought by several nations, among them the Japanese, who used them in considerable numbers in the Russo-Japanese war. The Russians were using Maxim guns, and this war was the first real testing ground for the machine-gun. It was the first time that two major powers, each armed with machine-guns, had come face to face, and the results were watched very closely by other nations. The Russians first used their Maxims at the Yalu River, where eight guns beat off several Japanese assaults and the Japanese, used to attacking en masse, were decimated.

They, in their turn, used their Hotchkiss guns with great boldness, carrying them

Hotchkiss Model 1914
The main French machine-gun of the First World War, this 8-mm strip-fed weapon, a redesigned version of the original 1897 Hotchkiss, was also sold to the US *Weight:* 55 lb *Rate of fire:* 450 rpm *Muzzle velocity:* 2400 fps

forward in the attack so as to give covering fire whenever needed. They were particularly adept at giving cover to an assault by firing over the heads of the attacking troops to keep down the defenders. As a result of their experiences the Japanese were well satisfied with the Hotchkiss design, and, having acquired a licence to manufacture them in Japan, they gradually improved the design by incorporating their own ideas.

The Russians were also using another machine-gun besides the Maxim. This was

Taisho 3
This Japanese machine-gun of 1914 was a
straight copy of the Hotchkiss Model 1914,
but incorporated a Lewis type of ejection system
Weight: 60 lb *Rate of fire:* 500 rpm *Muzzle
velocity:* 2434 fps

Imperial War Museum

the Danish Madsen gun, which formed
part of the armament of the Russian cavalry.
The Madsen is one of the most remarkable
machine-guns ever built. It was the first
which would be called, by modern standards,
a light machine-gun, and it was produced in
almost the same model for over 50 years.
It was used as an infantry gun, a tank gun
and an aircraft gun, and it was probably
one of the most complicated mechanisms
ever to achieve success. Yet it was never
adopted officially by any major power,
although it was used by 34 countries.

Sole success
The Madsen gun was designed by a Dane
called Schouboe, and was probably the only
one of his many weapon designs which was
a success. It was adopted by the Danish
cavalry in about 1902 and named after
Madsen, the then Danish Minister of War
who was particularly enthusiastic about
the weapon and had pressed hard for its
adoption by the army.
The mechanism of the gun is recoil-
operated and is best described as the
adaptation of the Martini rising breech
block to automatic action. When a round
is fired the breech block is aligned with the
barrel, and pins in the front end of the
block are riding in the forward end of a
groove in the 'Switch Plate', a track cut in
the side of the gun body. As the barrel and

*Left: French machine-gun emplacement,
spring 1918. Below: French infantry advance with their Hotchkiss Model 1914
near Montdidier, August 1918*

bolt recoil, the pin on the bolt is drawn through the groove on the switch plate, and the angle of the groove lifts the breech block clear of the chamber. A separate extractor, driven by a cam on the barrel, now extracts and ejects the cartridge case. As the barrel and block move back a firing hammer is cocked and a recoil spring placed under compression. When the rearward movement stops, the spring begins to force the moving parts forward again. The bolt pin, riding in the switch plate, is now moved by the angle of the switch plate groove so that the bolt is dropped below the level of the chamber, allowing a rammer unit to ram a fresh cartridge from the overhead magazine into the chamber. Then, as the barrel and bolt are about to complete their return, the switch plate moves the bolt up and closes the breech ready for the hammer to fall.

Thus, instead of the bolt simply moving back and forth and doing everything, in the Madsen the bolt simply closes the breech. Extraction, feed and ramming are all performed by other pieces of the mechanism. It is one of the most complicated devices ever seen, and yet it works without trouble most of the time. It does tend to balk a little at rimmed cartridges, and this is due to the path of the round as it enters the chamber; as the cartridge is forced in, it is slightly bowed or bent. But with rimless ammunition this seems to cause no trouble, and certainly if the Madsen were prone to problems it would hardly have survived as long as it did.

The Austro-Hungarian army was far from satisfied with its Skoda machine-gun, and in 1907 it adopted the Schwarzlose design. This was the invention of a German designer and, like the Skoda, dispensed with the formality of locking the breech block before firing the cartridge. Its operation relied entirely on having a massive breech block, backed up by a form of toggle joint which never actually locked the block but merely acted to slow down the opening movement. In order to get the breech pressure down quickly, the barrel was short – 20 inches against the Maxim's 28, for example – but due to the rather abrupt functioning of the gun it was necessary to lubricate the cartridges as they were loaded into the chamber so as to allow them to be extracted easily. The Schwarzlose was sold to Holland, Serbia, Bulgaria and Turkey, so it couldn't have been all that bad.

So far all the guns we have considered achieved some success, but by the early 1900s, when most of the major nations had made their minds up about what gun to adopt, things began to get harder for inventors. Even if they had a good design, they were up against guns which were tried and tested and armies which had already invested money and machinery in the gun of their choice. Sometimes they were hindered by a lack of resolution on the part of the people whom they hoped would buy.

One such designer was an Italian called Giuseppe Perino. Perino designed a machine-gun in 1900 and offered it to the Italian army. The gun was a very sound design,

German mountain troopers with a Madsen light machine-gun in Italy, 1917

Madsen
In spite of having one of the most complicated actions ever devised, the Danish Madsen 7·62-mm light machine-gun was used with great success by 34 countries over a period of more than 50 years *Weight:* 21 lb *Rate of fire:* 500–600 rpm *Muzzle velocity:* 2500 fps

Schwarzlose M07/12
This Austrian weapon was the only machine-gun with an unlocked breech to see widespread service use. The breech was held closed by a toggle lock which broke immediately upon firing, and like most blowback guns it needed a lubricated cartridge. Used in the First World War, it survived in the Italian and Hungarian armies until 1945 *Weight:* 44 lb (gun only) *Rate of fire:* 400 rpm *Muzzle velocity:* 2050 fps

Perino
The Italian Model 1908 machine-gun, this 7·7-mm strip-fed weapon was a victim of indecision by the Italian army and never entered service, although it was in many respects better than the guns that did *Weight:* 50 lb *Rate of fire:* 600 rpm *Muzzle velocity:* 2400 fps

SIA
This Italian gun was invented by Agnelli and made by Ansaldo, Armstrong & Co. It was a blowback gun, and Agnelli invented for it the idea of fluting the chamber so as to 'float' the cartridge on a layer of gas, and this helped the extraction. But it was counterbalanced by the open-sided magazine which allowed the cartridges to become coated with dust before they entered the gun. It was used as a training gun by the Italian army in the 1920s

A motorcycle-mounted Vickers machine-gun is used as an anti-aircraft gun in northern France

Imperial War Museum

using recoil augmented by the blast from the muzzle striking a fixed deflector to boost the recoil of the moving parts. Breech locking was done by a bell-crank system, and the recoiling barrel moved in a casing and functioned as a pump, directing a stream of cooling air into the breech area at every stroke. Feed was originally by a belt, but this was soon replaced by a tray system, a box on the side of the gun carrying a number of trays which were, in turn, taken into the gun.

In 1911 the gun was offered to various countries without success – they already had made up their minds about the guns they wanted – but the Italian army was still undecided. Under conditions of great secrecy they continued to test the gun, trying it against the Maxim, Colt, Skoda and any others they could find. Time went by and still they were unable to come to a decision. While they were still arguing the First World War broke about their heads, and they had to go out and buy whatever machine-guns they could find, since by that stage there was no time to think of setting up production facilities for the Perino. As a result, the Perino was never heard of again, and the Italians finished up with a handful of designs which were, in many respects, inferior to the Perino.

Another Italian venture is worth recording since it was responsible for an idea which has been used in many designs since. This was the SIA gun, designed by Giovanni Agnelli. The patents were taken up by the Societa Anonima Italiana G Ansaldo, Armstrong & Company (SIA) but although they produced one or two guns before 1914 they were unable to make much headway with the design until the 1920s. Eventually a few were sold to the Italian army who used them as training guns in the 1930s.

However, the interesting feature of the SIA gun was the method which Agnelli invented to simplify extraction. His design was for a blowback bolt, retarded by the

Vickers · 303 Mk 1
A modified Maxim, this water-cooled weapon was the British Army's standard medium machine-gun from 1912 to 1966 *Weight:* 40 lb *Rate of fire:* 450–550 rpm *Muzzle velocity:* 2440 fps

firing pin moving in a helical slot in the breech block. Like all blowback guns, extraction was violent, and the heads were frequently torn off the cartridge cases, leading to jams and stoppages.

Most inventors, when confronted with this, have resorted to lubricating the cartridge with oil or grease: this solves the problem but, of course, the oil coating acts as a magnet for dust and dirt, leading to more trouble. Agnelli solved it by cutting fine longitudinal grooves in the chamber of the gun, so that when it fired, some of the gas washed around the mouth of the case and entered the grooves. Thus, instead of the pressure on the inside of the case forcing the case tightly against the chamber wall to cause hard extraction, there was now an equal pressure on both sides of the case, and it was virtually floating in the chamber on a layer of gas. This made extraction quite easy, and since that time a grooved chamber has been recognised as the most likely solution to hard extraction with blowback guns.

By the time the Maxim gun had been in use for 20 years, it occurred to various designers that it could stand a little improvement. The first attempt appears to have been in 1909 when the German army demanded a machine-gun suitable for carrying in aircraft, and therefore lighter than the standard Maxim. The government arsenals could not devote staff or time to such a task, so a civilian company, the Deutsche Waffen und Munitionsfabrik of Berlin was given a development contract. Their designer, Heinemann, spent two years on the project and in 1911 produced the 'Parabellum' machine-gun. This was some 18 lb lighter than the Maxim, due to dispensing with the water jacket and redesigning the mechanism so that the toggle broke upwards. The barrel was enclosed in a perforated jacket which allowed air to flow round the barrel to cool it, and the gun was fitted with a shoulder stock and a pistol grip for aircraft observers.

It was a very good weapon and saw much service in the air. Had the army had sufficient forethought it would also have made an excellent light machine-gun for the infantry. As it was, when such a weapon was wanted, what the army got was simply the water-cooled Maxim minus its tripod.

The Vickers machine-gun
The other, and more famous, modification to the Maxim was the Vickers gun. This was a fairly simple re-design, involving turning the toggle upside down so that it broke in an upwards direction, and lightening some of the parts by the judicious calculation of stresses and the substitution of lighter metals.

The Vickers gun was introduced in November 1912 and remained in service with the British Army until 1968. It was a firm favourite with the army and performed some notable feats in its time. It had a maximum range of 4500 yards and could be fired, by using an optical dial sight, at targets out of direct view from the gun, the trajectory passing over intervening ground.

One famous episode was the barrage fired by ten guns of the 100 Coy, Machine Gun Corps on 24 August 1916, when almost one million rounds were fired. One gun fired 120,000 rounds without appreciable pauses and was working as perfectly at the end as it had been at the beginning.

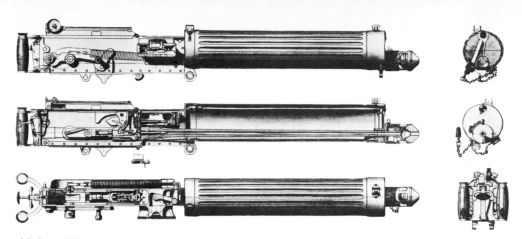

Vickers Mechanism
The basic Maxim design was modified by Vickers so that gas pressure in a muzzle cap helped force the barrel back, and the toggle joint broke upwards to open the breech. This illustration and those below are taken from the Vickers catalogue of 1914

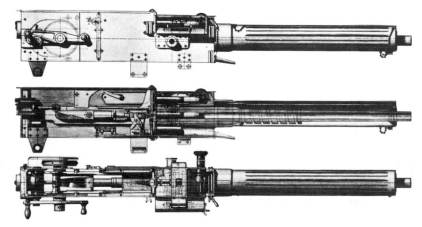

Vickers Naval 1-pounder
This weapon used the original Maxim toggle, breaking downwards, and a clock-type spring on the end of the crank. Note the heavy barrel return spring inside the jacket and the arrangements for ejecting the empty cartridge cases to the front. Maxim's basic mechanism was quite capable of dealing with ammunition of this size (37-mm) and even larger

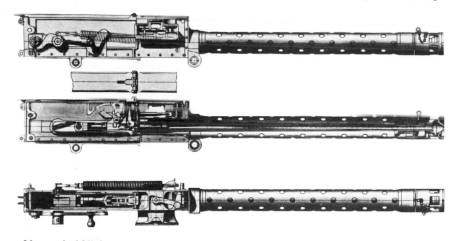

Air-cooled Vickers
The sectioned drawing in the centre shows how muzzle boost was achieved by the coned faces on the barrel and casting. The toggle lock was the standard Vickers pattern, breaking upwards to open the breech

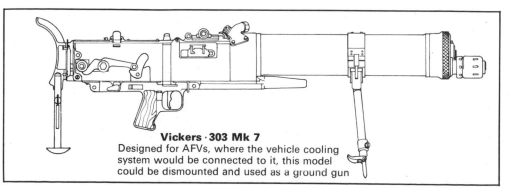

Vickers ·303 Mk 7
Designed for AFVs, where the vehicle cooling system would be connected to it, this model could be dismounted and used as a ground gun

When war broke out in 1914 the machine-gun was not present in great numbers. It is commonly believed that the Germans had thousands – one official American document published in 1919 says 50,000, which is a gross exaggeration – while the British and French had hardly any and were not particularly enthusiastic about those they did have. Like most legends, this is not precisely true. The Germans doubtless did have more, but only because they had a larger army. The allocation of machine-guns was exactly the same in the German, French and British armies – two guns per infantry battalion, so that there was little advantage on either side.

It was not until the war turned into a trench war that the machine-gun became prominent, and then largely because the Germans very astutely withdrew the guns from units in reserve and used them to thicken up the strength in the line. Very soon the machine-gun dominated the front, and each country was hard at work making all the machine-guns it could. This led to problems, for the machine-guns of the day were complex engineering jobs, demanding much precise machining and fitting and many hours of skilled work in their manufacture. The hunt began for more guns, and guns which could be made cheaply and quickly.

In the United States an inventor named Samuel MacLean had, with the aid of a Lt Col O M Lissak of the US Army, produced a design of gas-operated lightweight gun. Having no success in promoting it, he sold the patents to the Automatic Arms Company of Buffalo. They, in 1910, asked Col Isaac N Lewis, who had just retired from the US Army, to see if he could turn the design into a workable gun. In 1911 Lewis produced prototypes which he demonstrated to the Chief of Army Staff and the Secretary of War. Four guns were taken for study and there the matter rested; the Ordnance Corps made no attempt to follow up the matter at all, and Lewis finally went to Belgium and put the Lewis gun into production there. It was adopted by the Belgian army in 1913, and in 1914, when the war began, the British Army also purchased some, since the guns were, by that time, being made in England by the BSA company. After the outbreak of war the entire production capacity of BSA was employed in turning out Lewis guns, while contracts

THE FIRST WORLD WAR:

were given to the Savage Arms Company in America for more of them. By 1917 Savage were making 400 guns a week.

While the Lewis was a good ground gun, it became better known as an aircraft observer's gun. It appears that the first combat use of the Lewis in the air was on 22 August 1914, when two British pilots took a Lewis up and opened fire on a German Albatros, although without success. As well as being employed as a 'free' gun – that is, one which could be swung about freely by the observer – it was also used as a 'fixed' gun, mounted on the upper wing of the SE5 fighter, for example, and fired by a cable control from the cockpit. A quick-release mounting allowed the gun to be swung down by the pilot to change the drum magazine, and the positioning of the

gun allowed it to be fired outside the arc of the spinning propeller.

As a ground gun the Lewis showed some advantages which had not been considered before. In the first place, it could be made for about one-fifth the cost in time and material required for a Vickers gun; in the second place it was a good deal more portable and could easily be carried by one man in an assault, taking the firepower with him instead of leaving it behind to cover from a distance.

Slowly but surely the concept of the light machine-gun came into being. True, there was little chance for the concept to take much hold in the static war of the trenches, but when the opportunities for movement arose the advantages of a light-weight machine-gun could not be denied.

Lewis Gun
The first Lewis gun issued to the RFC was this 'Cut Down Mark One', which used a spade grip instead of a butt. This cutaway shows the piston and bolt at the rear of their stroke, about to chamber a fresh round. It also shows the cooling system of radial fins around the barrel over which air was drawn by the muzzle blast. Details from Army Code Book 60525, Handbook of Land Service Ammunition Part 1. Above: Breech and 47-round drum magazine of a Lewis gun *Weight:* 27 lb *Rate of fire:* 500–600 rpm *Muzzle velocity:* 2400 fps

THE LIGHTER MACHINE-GUN

The Lewis became famous as an aircraft gun; here, it is mounted at the front of a pusher-propelled DH 2

The Germans saw the same point: their first attempt at making a light gun was simply to take the Maxim '08 gun from its tripod or other mounting, fit it with a rudimentary bipod, and that was that – the '08/15 model. In spite of being heavy it had its advantages: it was a gun the soldiers all knew, it was reliable, and being belt-fed it could give sustained fire more easily than the drum-fed Lewis.

Shortly before the war the Bergmann Company, well-known gun makers, had offered a water-cooled machine-gun to the German army. This was actually designed by Louis Schmeisser, and later perfected by his son Hugo Schmeisser, a name which was to become far better known in connection with submachine-guns in later years. The design was good: the gun worked on recoil, a lock piece being cammed out of engagement with the bolt during the recoil movement. There was a quick-change barrel and a disintegrating link belt, both years ahead of their time.

But for all their excellence, only a few were adopted by the army as their Model 1910 machine-gun – they were reluctant to change from the Maxim. Later, under the pressure of war, they were glad to get all the Bergmann guns they could, and Bergmanns (doubtless due to Hugo Schmeisser) developed a lightweight air-cooled model which was taken into service as the Model 1915 nA (*neuer Art,* or new pattern). Late in the war it was fitted with a bipod and taken into use as a light machine-gun, but in numbers too small to have any useful effect.

A successful lightweight conversion of the basic Maxim, the '08/15 was simply the Model 1908 taken off its tripod and fitted with a bipod and shoulder stock. This reduced its weight to 38 lb, including water, making it better suited to mobile operations. Right: Maxim '08/15 mounted on outer envelope lookout position of a German airship about to set off on a raid.

After Louis Schmeisser developed the original model of the Bergmann machine-gun he left the company and worked for the Rheinische Metallwaren & Maschinenfabrik (Rheinmetall) of Düsseldorf. In 1901 this company had bought out the company formed by the famous designer von Dreyse, and in memory of him they named all their small arms 'Dreyse'. Louis Schmeisser now developed another design of machine-gun which was marketed as the Dreyse Model 1910. This was recoil operated and used a tilting breech block unlocked by cam tracks in the gun body. Originally a water-cooled gun, it was unable to make much headway against the established Maxim

'08 and few were seen in pre-war days, though once the war began the army took as many as Rheinmetall could turn out.

The French, who had by now realised the shortcomings of their St Etienne design, turned back to Hotchkiss for some machine-guns. By this time, though, Hotchkiss had redesigned their gun, improving it in many respects – although they still persisted with the strip feed system.

In 1909 they had changed the system of operation from the original locking plate to a new idea they called a 'fermeture nut'. Basically, this was a hollow nut with an interrupted thread cut on the inside surface. It fitted over the breech of the gun so that

Bergmann Model 1915nA
This 7·92-mm machine-gun, fed by a 200-round belt drum, might have replaced the '08/15 Maxim, but the pressures of war meant it was never produced in sufficient quantity
Weight: 34 lb *Rate of fire:* 750–800 rpm
Muzzle velocity: 2952 fps

the threaded portion received the head of the bolt as it closed. The bolt face had lugs on it which passed through the cut-away portions of the fermeture nut thread. The operation of the gas piston then rotated the nut so that the threads engaged behind the bolt lugs and locked bolt and barrel securely together. After the gun fired, the gas piston rotated the nut once more to unlock the bolt.

More of the same

In other respects the 1909 design was much the same as before – heavy and prone to overheat – and it was complicated by a redesign of the strip feed which now held the cartridges underneath the strip instead of on top. This model was adopted by the French in small numbers, and it was also taken into use by the US Army under the title of the 'Benet-Mercie Machine Rifle' and by the British as the 'Hotchkiss Machine-Gun Mark 1, Cavalry'.

It was not notably successful in any of these roles. The Benet-Mercie, in particular, received a slight setback to its credibility during the US border incidents involving Pancho Villa in 1916. Apparently Villa launched a raid on Columbus, New Mexico, one night. The garrison there had a Benet-Mercie, but did not fire it since, they claimed, it was too difficult to load in the dark – a rather poor recommendation.

The French army therefore settled for a supply of the Hotchkiss Model 1914. This was actually a slightly improved version of the Model of 1900, reverting to the bullet-up type of strip and modifying it so that strips could be hooked together to form a sort of

Italian troops in 1918 with a St Etienne, presumably given them by the French after Caporetto

belt feed, albeit not a very flexible one. But whatever else was wrong with the Hotchkiss, it was at least robust and reliable, and in the conditions of the First World War this was as much as most people cared to ask for.

With the British and Germans producing light machine-guns, the French decided that they too ought to produce something of the sort. Moreover, they were still enamoured of some pre-war tactical ideas, one of which was the 'assault at the walk', in which the infantry were expected to march across to the enemy position carrying machine-guns at their hips, spraying all before them. The Hotchkiss, turning the

scale at 52 lb, was hardly credible in this application, and the French army now formed a commission of firearms designers and instructed them to produce a light machine-gun or machine rifle. It was the worst day's work the army ever did.

There is a hoary old joke about the camel who wanted to be a racehorse but got designed by a committee, and the same sort of thing tends to happen in the firearms world when committees begin designing weapons. But rarely has any committee ever come up with anything so abysmal as the 'Chauchat' machine-gun of 1915.

Weltkriegsbücherei, Stuttgart

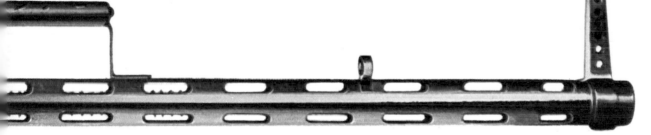

Chauchat Model 1915
Named after Colonel Chauchat, head of the commission that recommended its adoption by the French army, this was one of the worst machine-guns ever to see service. The 8-mm Lebel cartridge necessitated a semi-circular, 20-round magazine, and the long recoil operation, allied to shoddy construction, made it extremely unreliable. The US Army bought nearly 38,000 Chauchats; half of them were thrown away as useless by the troops
Weight: 18 lb *Rate of Fire:* 240 rpm
Muzzle velocity: 2300 fps

Browning Model 1917A1

After a brilliant demonstration of his gun's capabilities, Browning had his ·30 water-cooled gun accepted by the US Army. The A1 model, slightly modified from the original version, remained the standard US ground gun until the end of the Second World War
Weight: 41 lb *Rate of fire:* 450–600 rpm
Muzzle velocity: 2800 fps

Villar Perosa

This twin-barrelled light machine-gun, based on a 9-mm pistol cartridge, was so ineffective as a machine-gun that it was converted to a submachine-gun. The drawing is taken from the original patent; the photograph shows it on demonstration, with its carrying box and spares
Weight: 18 lb *Rate of fire:* 1500 rpm × 2
Muzzle velocity: 1200 fps

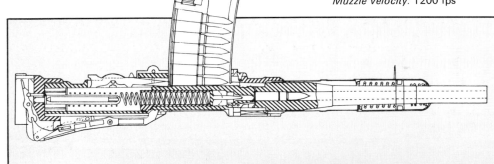

To begin with it was remarkable for the method of operation chosen – it was a 'long recoil' gun. In this system, rarely used except for a handful of pistols and generally unnecessarily complicated, the barrel and breech recoil together for a distance longer than the length of a complete round of ammunition. Having recoiled, the breech is then unlocked and the breech block or bolt is held still while the barrel is allowed to return to its normal position. There is now a large gap between the bolt and the barrel. The breech is then released and driven, by springs, towards the barrel, picking up a cartridge en route, chambering it and finally locking. The gun fires and the long recoil starts all over again. The cartridge case is extracted as the barrel is pulled away from the breech, and since the case is, in fact, standing still while the barrel moves away from it, there has to be a mechanically-driven ejector to knock the case out of the way.

It will be fairly evident from this description that a long recoil gun is going to be no bargain. The enormous movement of the gun causes vibration and prevents anything like an accurate aim being taken when firing automatic, and the movement of the barrel demands precise bearing surfaces, which soon get clogged with dust and dirt.

Fiat Revelli Model 1914
The bizarre feed arrangement was only one of the faults of this 6·5-mm weapon: its delayed blowback system of operation was rather too violent and an oil pump was needed to ease cartridge extraction *Weight:* 38 lb
Rate of fire: 500 rpm *Muzzle velocity:* 2080 fps

This could perhaps be tolerated if the gun were well built, but the Chauchat was thrown together from the cheapest materials and in the cheapest way.

While it fired the relatively low-powered 8-mm French cartridge it was marginally serviceable. But in 1917, when the United States came into the war, they were short of machine-guns, and as an interim measure they were persuaded by the French to buy 37,864 Chauchat machine-guns, having them chambered for the standard American ·30-06 cartridge. This was a much more powerful round than the French one, and the US Chauchats just about shook themselves to pieces. It has been said that over 50% of the American Chauchats were thrown away by the troops as being useless.

Believe it or not, the French were such good salesmen that they persuaded the Belgian and Greek armies to buy the Chauchat, renaming it the 'Gladiator'. However, the change of name did nothing to improve the gun's performance.

Although the Americans got the worst of the deal over the Chauchat, they were soon to overcome that setback with some designs of their own. But it took some organising, for the US Army had been slower in adopting machine-guns than any army in the world. In pre-war years it had bought machine-guns by the handful as and when it felt inclined or happened to have some spare cash. In 1916 a census of machine-gun stocks showed the following: 282 Maxim guns Model 1904; 158 Colt 'Potato Diggers'; and 670 Benet-Mercies.

As a result, the Secretary of War appointed a board of five officers and two civilians to study the subject and make recommendations. After considering the matter, the board recommended procurement of 4600

Vickers guns, and in December 1916 the War Department ordered 4000 guns from Colt, who had experience of making Maxim guns. They also purchased a number of Lewis guns from the Savage company, who had been making them on British contract.

The Lewis gun, in American service, had an odd career. It was firmly resisted by the Army, though the Navy and Marines adopted it. However, when the Marines got to France and came under Army control, the Lewis guns were taken from them and replaced with Chauchats. There has never been an official explanation for this, but evidence suggests that there was personal animosity between General Crozier, Chief of Ordnance, and Colonel Lewis. Crozier was an autocrat who never listened to the soldiers who had to use the weapons. He was bound and determined that they would have the weapons he considered best for them, a policy which resulted in the artillery, for example, having no American field artillery piece throughout the war.

For some unexplained reason Crozier took a dislike to Lewis and his gun, and until Crozier ceased to be the Chief of Ordnance the Lewis gun was a non-starter with the US Army.

But better things were in sight. After John Browning handed his gas-operated gun over to the Colt company, he went back to his drawing board and began again on a machine-gun design. This time he discarded

gas operation and, allowing that Maxim might have been right, began to work on a recoil operated gun. He took out his first patents for this in 1900, but the Army showed no interest and were unwilling to finance further development, so he dropped it and went to work for the Belgian Fabrique Nationale company on shotgun and pistol design.

In 1910 he returned to his home in Utah and took up the machine-gun once again, making some modifications to the original model. Again he could raise no interest, until February 1917, when Browning was invited to demonstrate his machine-gun. He produced the machine-gun and also a machine rifle or light machine-gun.

Impressive performance
The demonstration was successful and in May 1917, after the Declaration of War by the USA, a further test was made in which the machine-gun fired 20,000 rounds non-stop, at 600 rpm, then, after a pause, fired another 20,000 rounds just to show it wasn't a fluke. The inspecting board were unwilling to believe that this could be expected from run-of-the-mill production weapons, so Browning produced another gun, loaded it, and proceeded to fire it until he ran out of ammunition. After firing non-stop for 48 minutes 12 seconds and 28,920 rounds the gun stopped. Browning then got one of the spectators to blindfold him and proceeded to strip and re-assemble it.

As a demonstration it was masterly, and it did the trick; within weeks, contracts for 10,000 machine-guns and 12,000 automatic rifles had been placed. Unfortunately, it was a good deal easier to place orders than to make guns from scratch; drawings had to be prepared, tooling done, materials obtained. It was February 1918 before the first automatic rifles came from the factories, and April before the first machine-guns were seen. By the end of the war 40,438 machine-guns and 47,920 automatic rifles had been made.

The machine-gun and the automatic rifle operated on different principles, and in truth the automatic rifle would have been better called a light machine-gun – it was always employed as such – except that the US Army had been brainwashed by the French into acceptance of their hip-firing assault tactic.

The machine-gun operated by short recoil. The barrel and breech block recoiled together for a short distance until a locking lug was forced down and the breech block freed from the barrel. The barrel halted

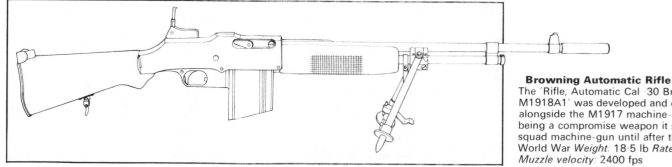

Browning Automatic Rifle
The 'Rifle, Automatic Cal ·30 Browning M1918A1' was developed and demonstrated alongside the M1917 machine-gun. In spite of being a compromise weapon it served as the squad machine-gun until after the Second World War *Weight:* 18·5 lb *Rate of fire:* 400 rpm *Muzzle velocity:* 2400 fps

Arming the first fighters

An RE 8 ready for takeoff in spring 1918, featuring an air-cooled Vickers on the fuselage side, synchronised to fire through the propeller, and a single Lewis on a Scarff mount

Vickers · 303 Mk 1*
The first Allied gun able to be synchronised to fire through propeller blades, this was a Mk 1 Vickers modified for air cooling with louvres cut in the barrel casing and belt containers for the ammunition *Weight:* 38 lb *Rate of fire:* 450–550 rpm *Muzzle velocity:* 2440 fps

Lewis Mountings
The Scarff mount (left), devised by Warrant Officer Scarff, RNAS, was adopted as standard by the RAF and remained in use until the start of the Second World War. Its main drawback was that if one gun jammed, it became almost impossible to fire the other. The earlier Foster mount (below) enabled the gun to be fired from the upper wing, over the propeller arc, by means of a cable

Spandau
Deriving its name from the factory in which it was made, this modified Maxim was the standard German fixed aircraft gun in 1915–16. It was no more than the Infantry Maxim '08 with an air-cooled barrel and perforated jacket and a lightened receiver casing. This cut the weight down to about 33 lb without impairing reliability

and an accelerator flung the bolt back against a spring. At the same time a transporter pulled a fresh round from the belt and placed it into a T-slot in the breech block face. The entry of the fresh round pushed the empty case out and allowed it to fall through a port in the bottom of the gun body. The block now came forward again, driven by the spring, chambered a round and locked to the barrel; then block and barrel ran forward to their original position. While they were still moving forward the cartridge in the chamber was fired. Thus, the explosion of the round had to expend some of its recoil energy in bringing the barrel to a halt before it could

start reversing it. This system of 'floating firing' is unique to the Browning and cushions the firing impulse so that the gun can handle powerful cartridges without excess strain.

The automatic rifle, on the other hand, was gas operated, since Browning considered this more applicable to light weapons. The gun was locked at the instant of firing by the rear end of the bolt being lifted up to butt against a step in the roof of the gun body. As the bullet passed up the barrel, gas went through a tapping and drove a piston backwards. This unlocked the bolt and carried it to the rear, extracting and ejecting the spent case. On the return

stroke the bolt picked up a fresh round from the bottom-mounted box magazine, chambered it and locked once more. Finally a hammer fell on the firing pin to fire the round.

The Browning Automatic Rifle was a good design in its way: the trouble was that it was neither one thing nor another. It was too heavy to be an automatic rifle, and too light to be a light machine-gun. As a rifle it was cumbersome to try and fire from the shoulder, and it needed a strong man to fire it with any degree of accuracy. As a light machine-gun it vibrated too much and the bottom-mounted magazine was inconvenient for changing in action. Nevertheless,

Parabellum
An early modification of the Maxim to provide a lightweight aircraft gun, the 7·92-mm Parabellum would have made an excellent ground gun *Weight:* 22 lb *Rate of fire:* 700 rpm

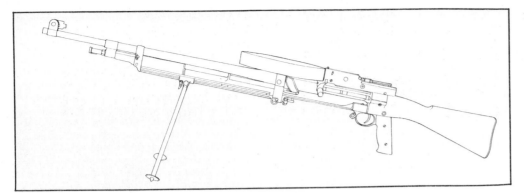

the US Army adopted it and kept it in service until after the Second World War. They admitted it wasn't the perfect light machine-gun, but they couldn't develop anything better.

With machine-guns for the ground forces under control, the US authorities now turned to the question of machine-guns for air use. The simple answer, and the one which was chosen, was simply to use the same design of Browning machine-gun but do away with the water jacket and make it an air-cooled gun. This was going to take some time to get into service, and in the interim the Marlin-Rockwell Corporation came up with a useful stopgap.

This company had been given a contract to make large numbers of the old Colt Potato-Digger for use as a training gun, and they had taken a good look at it and felt that it might be worth while redesigning it. They did this, doing away with the swinging arm and substituting a more normal gas piston mechanism, calling the result the Marlin machine-gun. Since the company was already tooled up to produce the Colt gun, and since it only required slight modification to the machinery to produce Marlin guns, the Marlin was accepted by the Army and went into production.

It turned out to have been a wise decision when it was realised that the Marlin was likely to be the only gun capable of being synchronised to fire through aircraft propellers until the Browning came along. Twenty-three thousand Marlin guns had been ordered, and after the guns had reached the front in France and proved their worth, this was increased to 38,000, and the whole of this contract was completed by October 1918.

The other major combatant in the First World War was Italy, and after their unfortunate episode with the Perino machine-gun they had been forced to take the Maxim and Vickers guns and put them into production as best they could. However, there was another native-made alternative before them.

In 1908 a Signor Revelli had designed a delayed blowback type of machine-gun, water-cooled and fed from a peculiar magazine system. This was a metal cage holding ten compartments of five cartridges each. As the gun operated the five rounds in the compartment were fired one by one, after which the whole unit moved over one step and presented the contents of the next compartment for firing.

The operation of the gun allowed the barrel and block to recoil together for about half an inch. The barrel then stopped and the block was free to move back driven by the force of the exploding cartridge; a swinging wedge device delayed the opening of the breech, but there was no positive lock. As a result, the breech opened abruptly and the extraction of the cartridge case was violent. In order to prevent the extractors tearing the rim of the case it was necessary to fit an oil pump to lubricate the cartridges as they were loaded, as with many blowback guns. Frankly, the Revelli was not a very good design, but it was simple and easy to make and soon became the standard Italian machine-gun, replacing the Maxim and Vickers as they wore out.

Late starters

In spite of the fact that the armies involved in the war now had plenty of experience and had decided on what machine-guns they wanted and had organised production, there were still plenty of inventors who were willing to try and improve on what already existed. Two of these are worth a mention, one British and one German.

The British gun was the Beardmore-Farquhar, which first appeared in prototype stage in 1917. It was designed by a Colonel M G Farquhar and built by the Beardmore engineering company of Birmingham. It was intended as an aircraft gun, was very light, and used an unusual method of operation. It was gas operated, with a normal gas piston, but instead of this piston working directly on the breech block, it loaded a spring. The pressure generated by the spring was carefully balanced to the pressure generated in the chamber when the gun fired, so that until the chamber pressure dropped the breech was securely locked. But once the pressure fell the spring could open the breech and begin functioning the gun. As a result the action of the gun was a lot less violent than usual and the weapon could be made that much lighter – it only weighed 16·25 lbs when loaded with a 77-round drum magazine.

Unfortunately, by the time the design had been perfected and was ready for testing, the war was over; one result of which was that the Royal Air Force looked much more critically at anything they were offered. Nevertheless the Beardmore gun worked very successfully and passed its tests. What really stopped it was the shortage of money and the general cutting of contracts which occurred in 1919 as the aftermath of war. There were hundreds of machine-guns in store and no justification for spending money on a new one, so the gun was turned down. It reappeared briefly during the Second World War, but by that time it had been overtaken by newer designs and it was not good enough for the changed conditions of aerial warfare.

The German gun was also intended as an aircraft gun. The principal difficulty with machine-guns used in aircraft was that their rate of fire was too slow. Even 600 rounds a minute was relatively poor when the pilot of a fighter only had the enemy in his sights for a fleeting second or two. In 1917 the German military authorities asked for designs of fast-firing guns which could be used in aircraft, and as a result of this the Vorwerk company of Barmen developed the Gast machine-gun. The gun was developed in great secrecy and was quite revolutionary in its mechanism. It consisted of two guns side-by-side, interconnected so that the firing of one gun operated the mechanism of the other. It was fed from two 180-round magazines which clamped on to the sides of the two gun units, and it delivered the phenomenal rate of 1800 rpm.

Had the development been pushed more actively, and the gun brought into service, it could have had a considerable effect on the war in the air. But the development was carried on very slowly and was not completed before the end of the war. The whole thing had been so secret that it was not for several months after the war had ended that the Allied Disarmament Commission heard about it, and it took even more time before they managed to obtain specimens for examination. A handful were eventually discovered and these were shared out among the Allies for tests. They all expressed themselves amazed at the weapon, but that was as far as they ever went. No further work was done on the design and only two or three specimens remain of one of the most remarkable guns ever built.

BETWEEN THE WARS: READY FOR A NEW ROUND

With the end of the war, development of machine-guns came to a halt for a time. Most of the countries involved now had a sufficiency of guns and were unlikely to require any for some years to come. But in the early 1920s one or two nations began to wonder whether they really had the best that was available and began to do some research. Probably the first to make a move were the French. This was understandable, since without doubt they had fought the war with two poor designs, the Hotchkiss and the Chauchat.

One of the stumbling blocks was the service cartridge, the 8-mm Lebel round. This was an ancient design – indeed, it had been the first military round to employ smokeless powder – and as well as being a poor performer it was a terrible shape to try and build an efficient machine-gun around. It was a rimmed cartridge with a sharp taper to the case, whereas the best shape for a machine-gun was a slender rimless round. The French began by copying the German 7·92-mm Mauser cartridge but, for reasons of their own, altering the calibre to 7·5-mm. Having got that out of the way, the next task was to design a machine-gun to suit, and this appeared as the Chatellerault Model 1924.

The Chatellerault owed a very great deal of its inspiration to the Browning Automatic Rifle, which had impressed the French when they saw it in use in 1918. The method of operation, by tilting the bolt to lock, was virtually the same, but the French designers were smart enough to move the magazine from the bottom of the gun to the top. This made the design a little more difficult but it certainly made the weapon easier to use in action. But the new cartridge was not particularly good, and the combination of Model 1924 and cartridge resulted in a series of mysterious explosions and defects which gave the gun a bad reputation.

The cartridge was later withdrawn and redesigned with a shorter case and the gun suitably modified, after which, in 1929, there was a fresh issue, the gun now being called the Model 24/29. This was much better, and the gun began entering service – very slowly, since the French taxpayers were more reluctant than any other to see money spent on their army. Most of the available money was going into the Maginot Line defences, and as a result there was a modified version of the Chatellerault called the Model 1931 which was specially designed for mounting in the forts. This used the same mechanism but had a longer barrel and a peculiar 150-round drum magazine mounted vertically at the side of the gun.

Other countries were attracted to the light machine-gun idea, but they took their time over it, having less pressing needs than did the French, and made a careful assessment of what was needed before they put pencil to paper. One of the prime requirements – which the French had ignored in their Chatellerault design – was that the barrel had to be capable of being changed rapidly.

Constant firing of a machine-gun soon warms the barrel to a very high temperature; 30% of the energy liberated when the cartridge is fired goes into heating the barrel. If a machine-gun is fired non-stop for a thousand rounds, the barrel temperature will be up in the region of 750–800°C, and this leads to trouble. The composition of the steel from which barrels are made is such that once the temperature gets to 550–600°C the molecular structure is affected and the steel begins to erode at an increasing rate. In a very short time, unless something is done, the barrel will be worn to such a degree that the bullets will no longer take the rifling and the gun's accuracy and long range disappear. In medium machine-guns this was taken care of by either putting a water jacket around the barrel, to transfer the heat to the water, or by making the barrel very heavy so as to give ample radiating surfaces. But in a light machine-gun these remedies were not acceptable, and the solution had to be a quick-change barrel, so that after firing a few

Chatellerault Model 1924/29
First developed in 1921, and bedevilled by accidents, this French 7·5-mm light machine-gun finally entered service in 1929 with new, rimless ammunition *Weight:* 22 lb *Rate of fire:* 450–550 rpm *Muzzle velocity:* 2700 fps

French troops off to defend their country with Chatellerault 24/29s, June 1940

hundred rounds the barrel could be quickly changed for a cool one and the hot barrel given a chance to cool down.

Shortly after the end of the war a French designer, Adolphe Berthier, produced a design of light machine-gun. It was gas-operated, using a tilting breech block and overhead magazine and with the barrel covered in cooling fins. He tried to interest his own government in the gun but they had committed themselves to the Chatellerault – which, in truth, wasn't very different in design to Berthier's gun – and he could raise no interest there. He therefore took the gun to England where it was adopted by the Vickers company and became known as the Vickers-Berthier.

During the 1920s the company turned these out in small numbers and sold them in various places, and as a result of comments from users they made a few changes. One of their first changes was to scrap Berthier's finned barrel and make a quick-change barrel instead. By grasping the barrel carrying handle and pressing in a catch, the barrel could be rotated and pulled from the gun body and a new barrel inserted in less than five seconds. After many trials the Vickers-Berthier was adopted by the Indian Army where it served reliably until well after the Second World War. Indeed, there is every likelihood that numbers of them are still in use with the Indian and Pakistan armies as training weapons.

Now the Indian Army of the 1920s was an independent entity which went its own way in the matter of weapons, although, of course, India was part of the British Empire. But there was a good deal of interchange of information and the good reports of the Vickers-Berthier were noted in the British War Office. By 1930 the British Army had begun looking for a new light machine-gun, since the Hotchkiss and Lewis guns they had were beginning to feel their age and, moreover, neither of them was exactly simple to operate and maintain. Nor did they have changeable barrels, and their cooling systems were archaic.

The Hotchkiss used a finned barrel, and it will be remembered that the early Hotchkiss guns were notorious for overheating. What happened was that in the course of normal cleaning and maintenance a slight film of oil was deposited on the barrel. Once the barrel warmed up the oil vaporised to give a shimmer of smoky heat currents above the barrel which effectively ruined any chance of accurate aiming.

The Lewis had one of the oddest systems

of cooling ever invented, though in all fairness it seems to have worked to some degree. The barrel was fitted with longitudinal fins and covered by a thin casing open at each end. The expansion of gas at the muzzle when the gun was fired induced a current of air to flow through the casing, across the fins, and so cool the barrel. How effective this was can be gauged by the fact that during the Second World War many ex-American aircraft Lewis guns were provided as ground light machine-guns. These had no cooling arrangements whatever, since they had been designed to be cooled by the rush of cold air caused by the aircraft's motion, and yet they gave no more trouble than the guns with complicated radiator systems.

Outsider wins
In 1932 a series of trials of possible replacements for the Lewis gun were held in Britain. The Vickers-Berthier was hot favourite, the Madsen was there, a new offering from Hotchkiss, a Swedish gun – whatever could be found was tried. One of the outsiders was a Czechoslovakian invention called the ZB26, a gun which had been seen by the British Military Attaché in Prague and reported on favourably by him. In the end, the ZB26 out-performed all the other competitors in accuracy, reliability and general ability, and negotiations began with a view to adopting it as the British LMG.

There was one slight flaw to be overcome: the ZB26 was chambered for the 7·92-mm Mauser cartridge, a rimless round, while the British Army, of course, was standardised on the rimmed ·303-in cartridge. This

meant a fundamental redesign of the weapon, and it speaks volumes for the ability of the Czech designers, Vaclav Holek and Anton Marek, that they were able to accomplish this without ruining the gun in the process. The outward and visible sign of change was the magazine. With rimless ammunition this was a straight-sided box, but to accommodate it to rimmed cartridges it had to be made in a curved shape.

The remainder of the modification went off well, and the new gun, known now as the ZGB33, was delivered to Britain for final tests. After the successful completion of the tests, arrangements were put in hand for manufacturing the gun at the Royal Small Arms Factory at Enfield. This took some time, but in September 1937 the first gun came from the production line there. Since the British Army had never gone in for the continental terminology system of dates and letters, it had to be given some sort of name, and it was called the Bren gun – BR from Brno, where the gun was designed, and EN from Enfield where it was built.

The Bren is probably the most successful and best light machine-gun ever made. As well as being used by Britain and all the Commonwealth armies – except the Indian, who stayed with their Vickers-Berthier – it was redesigned back into 7·92-mm Mauser calibre and built in Canada for the Nationalist Chinese army, and it was also used by the German army in the original ZB26 form. It rarely gave trouble, was simple to dismantle and maintain, was robust enough to withstand the hardships of battle and would keep on firing in conditions of mud, sand or ice which would stop many lesser guns. When the British Army abandoned the ·303 cartridge and adopted the 7·62-mm NATO round in 1956, the Bren was again reworked to take the new cartridge. This

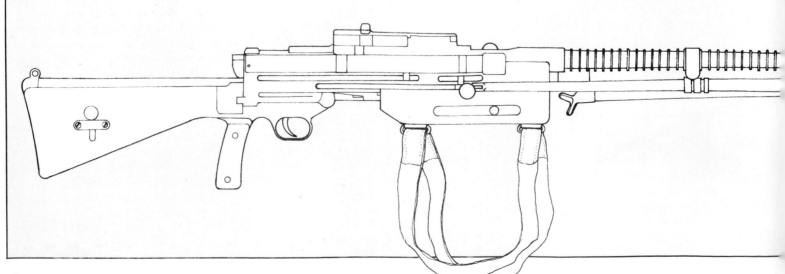

Besa Mark 1
This 7·92-mm gun was identical to the Czech ZB53 of 1937, and served as a tank gun with both the British and German armies
Weight: 47 lb *Rate of fire:* 450/750 rpm
Muzzle velocity: 2700 fps

Czech machine-guns: arming the world

time, though, the honoured name was dropped, since in the interim the Army had succumbed to the foreign habit of meaningless ciphers, and today the Bren gun is known as the Machine Gun L4.

The Italian Army also spent the 1920s looking for a light machine-gun. They had more need than anyone else, since they had fought a World War without one. Their standard weapon, as we have said, was the Revelli medium machine-gun, and in the search for something more convenient they had swung too far the other way and produced the Villar Perosa light machine-gun. This was a remarkable weapon which carried lightness to such an extreme that it is generally classed with the submachineguns. It was a delayed blowback weapon firing a 9-mm pistol cartridge, and it was always built as a double-gun unit controlled by a pair of spade grips at the rear end. Feed was from two overhead box magazines holding 20 rounds each, and as the rate of fire with both barrels working was in the region of 3000 rounds a minute, the operators soon became quite skilled at changing magazines.

Lightweight losers

These guns were so ineffective as light machine-guns that before the war was over the army had set two factories to the job of converting them back into submachineguns, in which application they were of rather more use. As a result the Italians still had nothing they could call a light gun, and in the search for a suitable weapon they managed to lumber themselves with some of the most appalling devices ever invented.

During the war the FIAT company, of motor car fame, had been given the job of making the Revelli machine-gun. To cope with the quantities demanded they had subcontracted some of the work to a company called SA Ernesto Breda, of Brescia, an engineering company whose previous products had been such things as locomotives.

In addition, FIAT set up a subsidiary firm in Turin, solely for making arms, called SAFAT. In the 1920s FIAT and Breda both decided to produce machine-guns. FIAT managed to supply aircraft guns to the Italian air force, then Breda obtained similar contracts, and finally it came down to a contest between them as to who would get the contract for the army light machine-gun. Breda won, and as a result FIAT decided to drop arms manufacture, and sold the SAFAT factory to Breda.

The Breda Model 1930 machine-gun, which the army adopted, was a curious weapon using a combination of recoil and blowback to operate it. The barrel and bolt were locked together by a fermeture nut similar to that of the Hotchkiss gun. On firing, the barrel and breech recoiled together for a short distance, during which time the fermeture nut was revolved by a cam on the gun body. Once the nut was unlocked, blowback threw the bolt clear, extracting the case, and then a spring drove the bolt back to chamber a fresh round. As the bolt reached the barrel, the two went forward together and the nut was revolved once more to lock. This system meant a very abrupt opening of the bolt and led to the usual trouble of blowback guns – difficult extraction. This was solved by the usual solution – an oiler fitted in the gun body which gave the incoming cartridges a thin coat of oil before they were loaded.

Hotchkiss FM 1922
This 7·5 mm French gun, built under licence, was the first product of Czeskoslovenska Zbrojovka Akciova Spolecnost v Brno, the Czech national armaments company which went on to supply many of the world's armies in the 1930s *Weight:* 19·25 lb *Rate of fire:* 550 rpm *Muzzle velocity:* 2250 fps

German troops in action with the Czech 7·92-mm ZB30 light machine-gun, France, 1940

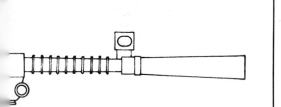

Vickers-Berthier
Designed by Adolphe Berthier and manufactured by Vickers, this ·303 light machine-gun was used by the Indian Army until after the Second World War *Weight:* 22 lb *Rate of fire:* 600 rpm *Muzzle velocity:* 2440 fps

Besal
This gun was designed by Harry Faulkner of BSA for easy mass production in case the Royal Small Arms Factory, the only supplier of Bren guns, was bombed. It was a brilliant design, but was never needed *Weight:* 22 lb *Rate of fire:* 600 rpm *Muzzle velocity:* 2440 fps

Bren Gun Mechanism
This cutaway shows the Bren at the instant of firing. The firing pin has been struck by the hammer, which forms part of the two-piece bolt unit. As the hammer unit went forward it cammed the rest of the bolt upwards to lock in front of a face in the receiver. When the gas piston moves back the hammer unit will retract first, unlocking the bolt, then the empty case will be extracted and ejected downwards

Bren Gun
The Mk 1 (above) and Mk 2 (right) versions of one of the most famous light machine-guns ever made were developed from the Czech ZB26, which was also used, in its original form, by the Germans *Mk 1 Weight:* 22·25 lb *Rate of fire:* 500 rpm *Muzzle velocity:* 2440 fps

Ghurka troops in action with a Bren light machine-gun during the battle for Tavoleto in Italy, 1944

Britain: the immortal Bren

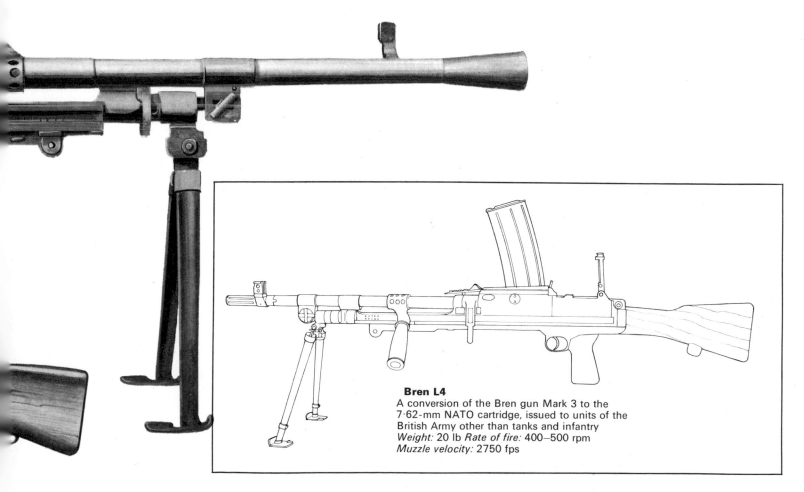

Bren L4
A conversion of the Bren gun Mark 3 to the
7·62-mm NATO cartridge, issued to units of the
British Army other than tanks and infantry
Weight: 20 lb *Rate of fire:* 400–500 rpm
Muzzle velocity: 2750 fps

The magazine arrangement was also peculiar, to say the least. It was a box magazine fitting horizontally on the right hand side of the gun, and was not detachable. However it could be unlocked and hinged to the front, so that it lay alongside the barrel, and the end of the magazine was then open so that clips of rifle ammunition could be used to load it. Once it was loaded the magazine was swung back and locked into place.

An Italian soldier with his Breda Model 1930. This gun had no carrying handle, so the gunner had to sling it on his shoulder or carry it in his arms

In theory this was good. It meant that the lips of the magazine, the most critical part of many guns, could now be machined into the steel of the gun body instead of being merely stamped into the metal of the magazine. Thus the feed lips would be protected and unlikely to be deformed or damaged, which was always a possibility with a detachable magazine. However, fixing the magazine to the gun also means that if any trouble develops in the magazine, the gun is out of action, so one must be balanced against the other. On balance, the disadvantages outweigh the advantages.

Another defect lay in the arrangements for supporting the barrel. Since it had to recoil, it had to be supported in bearings in an extended frame, and these bearings wore rapidly so that the barrel slopped about and became inaccurate. Moreover the sights were fitted to the gun frame, not the barrel, so when the barrel was changed (yes, it did have a quick-change barrel) there was no guarantee that sights and barrel were pointing at the same thing.

Frankly, the Breda M1930 was a terrible weapon – yet the army adopted it and continued to use it throughout the Second World War.

The FIAT company were persuaded to go back into the armaments business in the mid-1930s to try and produce a replacement for the ageing Revelli machine-gun, and they came up with their Model 1935. This was simply a Revelli with the water jacket removed, reliance being placed on air cooling of a heavy barrel. The peculiar compart-

Breda Model 1930
An awkward-looking 6·5-mm weapon with a peculiar hinged magazine fixed to the gun, which had to be filled from rifle clips
Weight: 20 lb *Rate of fire:* 500 rpm *Muzzle velocity:* 2080 fps

mentalised feed system was discarded and a more convenient belt feed adopted, and the oil pump was removed. In order to avoid trouble with extraction, FIAT went back to Agnelli's patent and cut grooves in the chamber to 'float' the case on gas and so ease extraction. Unfortunately they didn't do a very good job of it, and in spite of the fluted chamber the oil pump had to be re-fitted to ensure trouble-free firing.

Breda also produced a replacement for the Revelli, their Model 1937. This was an air-cooled, gas operated gun of modern appearance, but the smart exterior covered one or two mechanical aberrations.

In the first place, it seemed that Italian armament engineers were blind to the need to arrange their breech opening so as to give a slow and forceful unseating movement to the cartridge case before allowing things to speed up in order to pull the case cleanly out and eject it. All their guns opened violently, tearing at the case rims, and as a result, as we have seen, they always had to oil the cartridges before they were loaded. The Breda, which could easily have been designed with a slow 'primary extraction' movement, was just like all the others with a breech block opening suddenly, and thus it had to have the same old oil pump.

In the second place, the Breda goes down in history as having the craziest feed system ever introduced in a service weapon. The rounds were clipped into a steel strip, very much like that of the old Hotchkiss guns, which was entered into the right hand side of the gun body. The gun mechanism then extracted a round from the strip, loaded it, fired it, extracted the empty case from the chamber *and replaced it neatly into the strip* before indexing the strip across and withdrawing the next round. As a result the strip exited from the left side of the gun filled with empty cases.

In theory, these strips could now be put back in the boxes in which they had come, and sent back to somewhere or other for eventual refilling – a nice, tidy idea which must have had a good deal of appeal for the designer who dreamed it up and the armchair warrior who approved it. What happened in real life, of course, was that the sweating gunner and his assistant furiously stripped the empty cases out and threw them in all directions so that they could reload the strips, hoping that the enemy would not be so unkind as to interrupt them.

People have, in the past, been less than kind about the record of the Italian army in combat during the Second World War. There is food for thought in contemplating what they might have achieved had they been provided with some better weapons.

Improvements in Germany

By contrast, let us now turn to see what the German army were up to in the between-war years. They had finished the war with the venerable Maxim of 1908 and its 'light' offspring the Maxim '08/15, plus a collection of extemporised aircraft guns with bipods. There was room for a good deal of improvement here, and the Germans took their time about it.

Due to the restrictions of the Versailles Treaty there was little or no chance to manufacture machine-guns during the 1920s, and the Army spent their time profitably, thinking hard about the role of the machine-gun. Their conclusions were rather different from those of other people. They considered the machine-gun to be the basic squad weapon, about which the rest of the rifle squad revolved. Britain and France, on the other hand, looked upon the riflemen as the basic unit, and the machine-gun as a back-up for them.

Italy: among the world's worst

Breda Model 1937
This 8-mm replacement for the FIAT Revelli was marred by several odd mechanical features, including a feed system which replaced empty cartridge cases in their strips *Weight:* 42·5 lb *Rate of fire:* 500 rpm *Muzzle velocity:* 2600 fps

Mauser MG-34
Developed from the MG-30, this 7·92-mm weapon probably served in greater numbers than any other gun during the Second World War
Weight: 24·5 lb *Rate of fire:* 750 rpm
Muzzle velocity: 2750 fps

Because the Germans placed the main emphasis on the machine-gun, they arrived at a different opinion as to what the machine-gun should be. They could see no justification for dividing guns into medium or light models, since, in their proposed system of employment, either gun might be called upon to fight in either role. What was wanted, therefore, was a gun light enough to be called a light machine-gun and accompany the rifle squad anywhere, but heavy enough to be capable of laying down sustained fire for defensive purposes if needed. What they wanted, in fact, was a general purpose machine-gun. But nobody had thought of calling it that, and the name didn't appear for another thirty or so years.

Due to the Versailles Treaty the German gun-making firms had made various secret alliances with foreign companies in order to keep their design staffs occupied, and one of the companies with such connections was the Rheinmetall firm. They had bought up a moribund Swiss engineering firm called Solothurn, and they had also acquired a controlling holding in an Austrian company, Steyr. As a result, designs went on paper in Düsseldorf, were engineered by Solothurn and put into production by Steyr, being then marketed by a sales organisation called Steyr-Solothurn AG of Zurich.

One of the first weapons to appear from this devious pathway was the Solothurn MG-30, which the Swiss company offered to the German army in 1930. It had, of course, been designed by Louis Strange of the Rheinmettal company, and was a very

German troops loading and firing their MG-34 during the invasion of France, 1940

advanced design which used barrel recoil to drive back the bolt which was then rotated to unlock by two rollers running in cam tracks in the gun body. It was a very slender gun, the butt being in prolongation of the body and giving a 'straight line' configuration, which delivered the recoil in a straight line to the firer's shoulder and thus prevented the gun from rising as it fired. It incorporated an ingenious quick-change arrangement for the barrel in which the butt was twisted through 90° and pulled off. The bolt and barrel could then be withdrawn through the gun body and a fresh barrel slipped in place.

About 5000 of these guns were made, most of which were bought by Austria and Hungary, and the German army only took a small number. Good as it was, they thought it could be better, and they passed some samples of the gun over to the Mauser company with a request for improvement.

When Mauser had finished 'improving' the MG-30 it bore little resemblance to what they had started with. They got rid of the side-feeding box magazine and made the new design a belt-fed weapon which, by quick substitution of a different top cover, could also use a 75-round double drum magazine. The bolt locking system was altered so that only the bolt head revolved, locking by interrupted threads; an additional recoil impulse was given to the

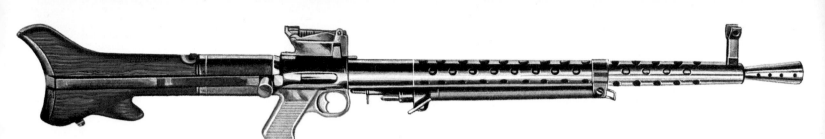

barrel by adding a muzzle gas trap; the quick-change system was altered by hinging the gun body to the back end of the barrel casing, so that the body could be unlatched and swung sideways to allow the barrel to be pulled straight out of the casing; and the trigger was designed as a rocking unit so that pressure on the top half gave single shots while pressure on the bottom section gave automatic fire at the high rate of 850 rounds per minute. The resulting weapon was known as the MG-34 and became the German army's standard machine-gun.

The MG-34 only had one defect: it was too good. The quality of the design and workmanship meant extremely precise and long manufacturing processes, and the tolerances on the weapon were so fine that it was easily upset by dust and grit. Manufacture was so difficult that eventually, during the war, there were five factories doing nothing but turn out MG-34s as hard as they could go, plus a number of other factories doing nothing but manufacture component parts. By 1941 this was obviously impractical and something new had to be designed, but nevertheless the MG-34 remained in production and use until the war ended. It has been estimated on good authority that there were probably more MG-34s in use during the war than any other single model of gun.

The rapid expansion of the German army in the 1930s moved faster, at first, than the

Germany: the general purpose machine-gun

Solothurn MG-30
Produced by the Swiss subsidiary of Rheinmettal, this was an excellent, though expensive, design with several advanced features. Only a few were bought by the German army. *Weight:* 17 lb *Rate of fire:* 800 rpm *Muzzle velocity:* 2500 fps

gun-makers could provide for, and as a result the German soldiers were frequently to be seen using odd weapons which did not figure in the inventories for very long. Also, as the Third Reich expanded its borders the army was able to assimilate various foreign guns into its own service, and in this way it managed to train its soldiers until there were sufficient of the MG-34 to go round. Many of the odd guns remained in use throughout the war, for even with all-out production there was never sufficient supply

German troops with MG-34 general purpose machine-gun in action in Russia

of the best weapons to permit getting rid of the merely serviceable ones.

It has already been said that both the British and German armies used virtually the same gun, the British having the Bren and the Germans the ZB26, but there was another Czech design which also appeared on both sides under different names. The Czechs called it the VZ37, the Germans the MG-37(t) and the British called it the Besa. Whatever name it was travelling under it was the same gun, developed in the early 1930s and put into production in 1937. It was designed by Holek as a tank gun, having a very heavy barrel, and was gas operated with recoil assistance. The barrel and bolt recoiled a short distance, after which a gas piston unlocked and opened the bolt.

The design was, of course, in 7·92-mm calibre and it was offered to Britain in late 1937 when time was getting short. Instead of changing the design to ·303, as was done with the Bren, the British Army decided to keep it at 7·92 mm so that it could go into production straight away, and manufacture a special supply of 7·92-mm ammunition for it. This was less of a problem than might be thought at first sight, since because the guns were limited to use in tanks it was not too difficult to set up a separate ammunition supply line for them, a thing which would have been impossible had the gun been on more general issue.

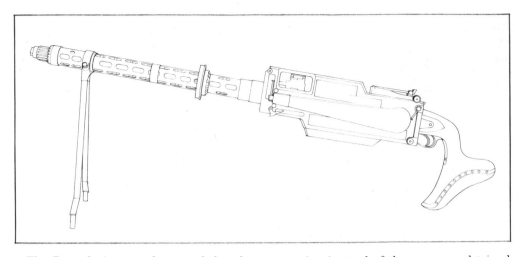

Maxim-Koleshnikov
An early Russian light machine-gun, this lightened and modified Maxim Model 1910 was not very successful when used in the Spanish Civil War *Weight:* 38 lb *Rate of fire:* 500–600 rpm *Muzzle velocity:* 2800 fps

The Besa design was later scaled-up by the BSA company to 15-mm calibre to provide a very heavy machine-gun for armoured cars. This fired a 2·5-oz bullet at 450 rpm and could penetrate an inch of armour plate – quite a formidable weapon.

In the German army the VZ37 became a tripod-mounted heavy machine-gun. Since 7·92-mm was the standard German cartridge there was no problem in that quarter and the Germans took the full production of the weapon throughout the war.

Russian re-think

One reason for the enormous German appetite for machine-guns was, of course, their ill-fated invasion of Russia, and it will be as well for us to look now and see what the Russians were doing in the machine-gun world. Their only machine-gun during the First World War had been their Maxim Model 1910, which was just like anybody else's Maxim except that it was heavier. While the British Vickers weighed 32·5 lb and the German Maxim '08 40·5 lb, the Russian Maxim weighed in at 52·5 lb, plus another 110 lb for its unusual wheeled mounting. Doubtless this massive construction aided reliability, but it certainly made it a handful to move about, which is probably why the Russians developed their wheeled

mounting instead of the more usual tripod mount. But 162·5 lb, without water or ammunition, was no sort of a joke even for a husky Cossack, and something lighter was desperately needed.

The first attempts appear to have been based on the German Maxim '08/15 con-

version, simply a matter of taking the basic Maxim mechanism and building a lighter gun around it. In this way the Maxim-Tokarev and Maxim-Koleshnikov guns were produced in the middle 1920s. Both were simply air-cooled barrels in perforated jackets on the front of the usual Maxim body, with wooden shoulder-stocks, pistol grips and simple bipods. Neither was particularly successful and they were eventually disposed of, most of them being sent to Spain during the Civil War.

In 1921 a Soviet designer called Vasily Degtyarev began work on a design of light machine-gun. This was adopted for service in 1926 as the DP – *Degtyarev Pekhotnii* or Degtyarev Infantry – model. Production did not begin immediately, but was delayed until 1932 or 1933, and the first real test of these guns was in the Spanish Civil War.

The DP was a gas-operated gun which fed from a 47-round drum on top, and the bolt-locking system was a very simple adaptation of a Swedish invention in which two flaps were pushed out from the bolt by the

Left: Russian partisans with a Degtyarev DK heavy machine-gun with its flash-hider removed. Below: A lend-lease Russian Sherman with DT tank machine-gun enters Berlin with a Maxim Model 1910 on its back

Degtyarev DP
The main Russian light machine-gun of the Second World War, enormous quantities of this 7·62-mm weapon were built, and it is still in widespread use *Weight:* 20 lb *Rate of fire:* 500–600 rpm *Muzzle velocity:* 2770 fps

Russia: replacements for the Maxim

movement of the firing pin. This system proved to be very resistant to dirt and dust and the gun was extremely reliable, even though it looked quite slender and fragile. The only serious defects were in the positioning of the recoil spring under the barrel, where the heat drew its temper and softened it during prolonged firing, and the design of barrel-change which involved removing the bipod and gas cylinder before the barrel could be taken off. Nevertheless the DP was the Red Army's primary infantry gun throughout the Second World War.

A modified version was produced in 1944 in which the return spring was removed from its position under the barrel and placed in a tubular housing which protruded from the rear of the gun body, over the butt. This meant that the firer could no longer grip the small of the butt to squeeze the trigger, and a pistol grip had to be fitted. Another improvement was the strengthening of the bipod and changing its mounting point to the barrel jacket, which improved the gun's stability and also made barrel changing easier.

While the Maxim 1910 was kept in service – there were plenty of them, there was plenty of manufacturing capacity, and they were reliable – it was also thought advisable to develop another heavy machine-gun design. Degtyarev was assisted in this by G Shpagin, the result being called the DShK – Degtyarev Shpagina Krasnoi (Krasnoi meaning 'heavy'). This was a 12·7-mm gun, air-cooled, using the same gas-driven flap locking system as the DP.

Shpagin's contribution was the feed system, an unusual combination of belt and rotary feed. Above the bolt of the gun is a rotary unit into which the belt is fed; this revolves rather like the cylinder of a revolver and strips the rounds from the belt, discarding the links as it does so. As the unit indexes round the movement of the bolt it takes the round from the bottommost division at each stroke, ramming it straight through the unit and into the breech. While this is a serviceable system – in spite of its complexity – it took a skilled gunner to deal with it if it happened to jam, and after the war it was scrapped, a more simple system of levers being used instead and the gun being known as the DShKM (M for Modified).

The DShK turned out to be too big and heavy for use in the infantry role, though it was a highly successful anti-aircraft machine-gun and was also frequently seen on tanks. So another attempt had to be made to find something to replace the Maxim, and another designer, Goryunov,

was invited to try his hand at a solution.'

The Goryunov, or SG43 machine-gun, was one of the best air-cooled machine-guns ever devised, and it is still in service with the Soviet Army at the time of writing. Gas operated, the bolt is locked by a sideways movement into a recess in the gun body. The barrel can be quickly changed and the feed is from a belt. At the time this gun was developed the standard Soviet cartridge was still the old 7·62-mm rimmed round which originated in 1891 with the Mosin-Nagant rifle. As a result the round has to be pulled backwards out of the belt, lowered, and then rammed into the breech. In spite of this apparent complication the feed system gives no trouble and the gun is extremely reliable on all counts.

Japanese conservatism
Another nation which was to be involved in the Second World War and whose machine-guns needed overhaul was Japan. The Japanese had, as we have already mentioned, adopted the Hotchkiss gun in 1902, and since the Japanese army were somewhat conservative in the matter of equipment, the Hotchkiss gun was their

Degtyarev DShK
This 12·7-mm heavy machine gun first appeared in 1938 and was used throughout the Second World War as an anti-aircraft gun. It later saw service in Korea *Weight:* 73·5 lb *Rate of fire:* 550–600 rpm *Muzzle velocity:* 2763 fps

Type 99
This widely-used 7·7-mm machine-gun was developed in 1939 from the Type 96, with a new round of ammunition intended to eliminate the need for lubrication *Weight:* 23 lb *Rate of fire:* 850 rpm *Muzzle velocity:* 2350 fps

standard from then on: no matter what they designed or built, it still came out looking like a Hotchkiss.

Their first postwar gun was the Taisho 11 Model, and before going any further it might be as well to explain the Japanese system of naming and numbering their weapons. There were two basic systems in use, both of which had reference to the year of the gun's introduction. The first system referred to the year of the reign of the Emperor at the time of introduction: Taisho 11 refers to the 11th year of the Taisho Era, which in the Western calendar was 1922. In 1926 the Showa Era began, so that a weapon introduced in 1940 would be 'Showa 15 Model'. The other system also referred to the calendar but to the Japanese calendar which, by Western reckoning, began in 660 BC. Thus the Type 92 Machine-gun (notice the absence of any qualifying era name such as Taisho or Showa) refers to the Japanese year 2592, or 1932 in Western terms. Having got that clear we can now go back to the Taisho 11 gun, which came into service in 1922.

This gun was designed by Colonel Kirijo Nambu, the noted Japanese firearms expert. The basic Hotchkiss gas operation was retained but an unusual feed system was

employed. This comprised a square hopper on the left of the gun into which six five-round rifle chargers could be dropped, lying on their sides with the bullets pointing forward. As the gun fired, so the cartridges were stripped from the bottom charger, the empty charger being discarded and the next one falling into place. This system allowed any rifleman to provide ammunition for the squad weapon, and it also meant that the gun could be constantly topped up while firing was in progress, there being

no need to stop firing to change magazines. In practice, however, it was found that the standard rifle round was rather too powerful for the gun and a special reduced-charge cartridge had to be provided for it, which rather cancelled out most of the theoretical advantages.

Another fault of this weapon was that the bolt opened very abruptly and jerked the empty case out of the breech without first applying a primary extraction impulse. As we have seen with Italian guns, this fault can lead to split and separated cases, and the Japanese adopted the same solution as the Italians, adding an oil reservoir to lubricate the rounds as they were fed to the breech.

To provide something heavier, Nambu now set about redesigning the Taisho 3 gun of 1914 which was, in fact, the French Hotchkiss Model 1914. Again, Nambu's principal contribution was a retrograde step, for he managed to redesign the mechanism to do away with the gradual opening of the breech, so that the usual oiler had to be incorporated.

The standard Japanese cartridge had been a 6·5-mm round for many years, but experience in China led them to consider changing to something heavier, and in 1932 a 7·7-mm cartridge was adopted which was more or less a copy of the British ·303 round. After this quite logical step they went mad and developed three totally different cartridges in the same calibre, one rimmed, one rimless, and one semi-rimmed. There has never been a satisfactory explanation of the reasoning which lay behind this extraordinary decision, one which must have given Japanese quarter-masters quite a headache.

As a result of this change it became imperative to produce some machine-guns to suit, and the first to be changed was the Taisho 3, after which it became known as the Type 92. There was very little basic change. In fact the internal mechanism remained the same – even to the oiler – though the external appearance was changed by the addition of a flash hider to

Japanese troops during the conquest of the Pacific with Taisho 3 copy of the Hotchkiss Model 1914

Type 92
Known as the 'Woodpecker' from its peculiar stuttering noise, this 7·7-mm medium machine-gun was an improved version of the Taisho 3 (Hotchkiss) using a new type of ammunition *Weight:* 61 lb *Rate of fire:* 500 rpm *Muzzle velocity:* 2400 fps

Type 96
Based on the ZB26 forerunner of the Bren, this 6·5-mm light machine-gun had a cartridge oiler incorporated in the magazine *Weight:* 20 lb *Rate of fire:* 550 rpm *Muzzle velocity:* 2400 fps

Japan: sticking with the Hotchkiss

the muzzle and a peculiar double pistol grip to the rear end.

The worst thing about it was its weight – 122 lb on a tripod. As a result the tripod was made with two sleeves on the front legs into which carrying poles could be fitted for two men to support, while the third man on the gun team fitted a carrying yoke, like a pair of overgrown bicycle handlebars, to the rear leg. In this fashion the three men

China, 1937: Japanese machine-gunner in action with Taisho 11 light machine-gun

could carry the gun and tripod fairly quickly without having to dismantle it. The Type 92 was the most common medium Japanese gun during the Second World War. It had a slow rate of fire – 450 rpm – and its distinctive noise led to its nickname of 'Woodpecker' among Allied troops.

The Japanese recognised that the Taisho 11 was not all that it might be, and in 1936 they produced a fresh design, intended to replace the earlier gun. This was the Type 96, but due to their poor organisation for production it never appeared in sufficient numbers to completely oust the Taisho 11, which stayed in service until 1945.

The Type 96 was based on the same mechanical action as the Taisho 11, but one or two features appeared which look as if they were copied from some of the Czechoslovakian ZB guns which the Chinese were using against them. The most important change was to discard the hopper feed and use a more conventional top-mounted detachable box magazine. One

odd feature was the fitting of a bayonet boss on the gas cylinder so that the gun could be decorated with the standard Japanese army bayonet. This was probably quite useless as an offensive weapon, but it may have had some virtue in keeping the muzzle down and thus making the gun steadier.

The cartridge oiling system was also discarded, but since the mechanism was unchanged, the rounds still had to be lubricated, and this was now done by a combined magazine loader cum lubricator. This, of course, made things worse. Previously the cartridge could pick up dust only while it was in the gun. Now the gun crew were running around with pouches full of oily cartridges, allowing ample time and opportunity for dust and grit to settle on them. It can come as no surprise to find that the weapon handbook listed no less than 26 different kinds of stoppage that the gun might suffer from.

Finally, with the adoption of the 7·7-mm cartridge, Japan had to produce a light

Taisho 11
This Nambu design of 6·5-mm light machine-gun was fitted with a hopper intended to be fed with Arisaka rifle ammunition clips, a good idea in theory but one which did not work in practice *Weight:* 22·5 lb *Rate of fire:* 500 rpm *Muzzle velocity:* 2300 fps

Browning · 50 Heavy Barrel M2
Originally developed as an aircraft weapon,
the Browning M2 was brought into use with
ground troops as a possible anti-tank gun
and later as a general heavy support weapon.
It has been widely used in the anti-aircraft role,
and is still to be found in service with armies
all over the world *Weight:* 84 lb
Rate of fire: 500 rpm *Muzzle velocity:* 2950 fps

The United States: Brownings all the way

machine-gun to take this round. Called the
Type 99, from its introduction in 1939, this
was little more than a Type 96 in the new
calibre, but at last somebody saw the light
and redesigned the breech opening cams
so that there was, at last, adequate primary
extraction. So for the first time the Japanese
now had a gun that did not need oiled
ammunition. As a result it was one of the
best weapons they ever produced. Again,
while the intention was to replace the earlier
Taisho 11 and Type 96 guns, their production facilities were so poor that they never
got anywhere near this, and all three guns
served side by side throughout the war.

The American Army were well satisfied
with their Browning machine-gun and
Browning automatic rifle which the First
World War had produced, and their only

*Flying Fortress crewmen pose in front of their
aircraft, with its heavy nose armament of ·50-cal
M2 Brownings. The original armament of the
Fortresses proved inadequate, and was rapidly
beefed up with more and bigger guns*

Browning · 30 M1919A4
Shown on the 'Mounting, Tripod M2', a
standard combination used as an infantry support
gun, carried as auxiliary equipment in combat
vehicles and used by cavalry in pack-mounted
form. The traverse and elevating mechanism
could be unlocked to allow the gun to swing
freely or clamped and used for firing on fixed
lines at night *Weight:* 31 lb *Rate of fire:* 500 rpm
Muzzle velocity: 2800 fps *Horizontal arc:* 50°
Vertical arc: from −21° to +19°

Browning · 30 M2

change during the inter-war years had been
to adopt an air-cooled Browning model in
·30 calibre and a heavy ·50 Browning as a
tank and anti-aircraft machine-gun. This
began as a water-cooled model but an air-
cooled model was also developed. The air-
cooled guns had come, in the first place, as
aircraft weapons, but some trials had
shown that they were quite suitable as
ground guns as well, and eventually the
air-cooled models completely replaced the
water-cooled ones.

The Browning automatic rifle was still
used as the squad light machine-gun, but
its defects in this role were somewhat
concealed by the fact that in 1936 the Army
adopted the semi-automatic Garand rifle
as the standard infantry rifle, and the
firepower produced by a squad of men
armed with this weapon more than made up
for any shortcomings of the BAR. Nevertheless, it is interesting to speculate on what
the American Army might have done had
the Garand been backed up by a decent
light machine-gun.

Breda Safat Model 1935
The free version of this 7·7-mm aircraft gun
weighed 27 lb and had a rate of fire of 800 rpm

Mauser MG-81
This twin 7·92-mm aircraft gun was based on
the MG-34, and with a muzzle recoil intensifier
produced 1250 rpm, making it very suitable for
aircraft use

*German aircraft gunner with his
hand-held MG-15 machine-gun*

Der Bordschütze
Er späht nach Sowjetjägern. Oft
hält er auch mit den Feuerstößen

AIRCRAFT MACHINE-GUNS

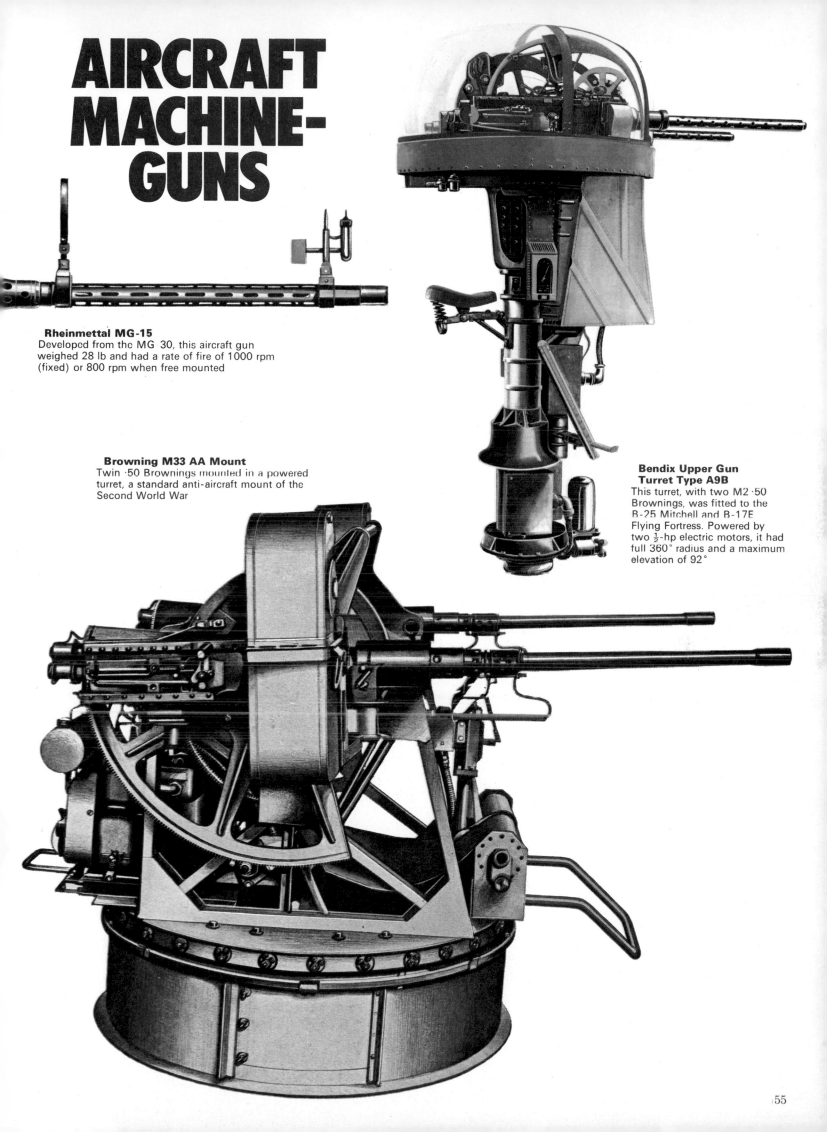

Rheinmettal MG-15
Developed from the MG-30, this aircraft gun weighed 28 lb and had a rate of fire of 1000 rpm (fixed) or 800 rpm when free mounted

Browning M33 AA Mount
Twin ·50 Brownings mounted in a powered turret, a standard anti-aircraft mount of the Second World War

Bendix Upper Gun Turret Type A9B
This turret, with two M2 ·50 Brownings, was fitted to the B-25 Mitchell and B-17E Flying Fortress. Powered by two $\frac{1}{2}$-hp electric motors, it had full 360° radius and a maximum elevation of 92°

When war broke out in 1939, then, everybody was well satisfied with their machine-guns, though, of course, they were all in need of vastly greater numbers as the war progressed. Britain, relying on only one factory for the production of the Bren gun, was in a delicate position, and after the fall of France the British Army had to turn to the USA and buy whatever they could find there. The result was the addition of several hundred Lewis guns to the British stocks. These were used as Home Defence weapons for the Regular Army and Home Guard, so that the Bren production could go to units fighting overseas. Another arrival from America was a large quantity of old Marlin machine-guns which had been superseded in US aircraft by the Browning. These were mostly used as anti-aircraft machine-guns on merchant ships.

Nevertheless, the concentration of Bren production under one roof was a great worry – one good air raid on Enfield and there would be no Bren guns for a while. So in 1940 BSA were asked to design a 'utility' Bren gun which could go into immediate production should anything happen to curtail Bren supplies. They quickly developed the 'Besal' gun, a brilliant design in which cheapness and speed of manufacture were the primary considerations. The body of the gun was made of steel pressings, the piston was square-section so that no time-consuming lathe work was needed, and the bolt was a simple square piece of metal. It fed from a top-

THE SECOND WORLD WAR: QUANTITY NOT QUALITY

Rheinmettal MG-3
A developed version of the MG-42, the 7·62-mm MG-3 is now the standard general purpose machine-gun of the German Federal Republic's armed forces *Weight:* 24 lb *Rate of fire:* 600/1200 rpm *Muzzle velocity:* 2750 fps

German troops with MG-42, Monte Cassino, 1944

Krieghoff FG-42
The 7·92-mm *Fallschirmjäger Gewehr* (paratrooper's rifle) combined the accuracy of a rifle with the firepower of a light machine-gun *Weight:* 14 lb *Rate of fire:* 400—450 rpm *Muzzle velocity:* 2750 fps

The MG-42 in its sustained fire role

Mauser MG-42
Developed from the MG-34 and known to Allied troops as the Spandau, this 7·92-mm weapon was one of the best general purpose machine-guns and has provided the basis for many subsequent weapons *Weight:* 24 lb *Rate of fire:* 1200 rpm *Muzzle velocity:* 2750 fps

mounted magazine, using the Bren magazine in fact, and cocking was done by pulling the pistol grip to the rear.

It performed excellently on trial, and one is inclined to wonder why the government had failed to put the same problem to BSA ten years earlier and saved themselves a lot of trouble over the Bren gun. Once the design was approved, drawings were made and jigs and tools produced, and then the whole project went into mothballs ready for the day when it would be needed. It never was, since Enfield was never prevented from turning out Bren guns, and the Besal passed into history. Due to confusion with the already existing Besa gun, the Besal was rechristened the Faulkner gun, taking its name from the designer, Mr Harry Faulkner of BSA.

The only other British machine-gun design to appear during the war was a private venture by, of all people, Rolls-Royce, who came into the gun business by way of their normal interest in aircraft. There was, in 1941, a bottleneck in supply of the ·50 Browning machine-gun, and Rolls-Royce decided to design a suitable gun for use in bomber turrets. One requirement was that the gun should be shorter and lighter than the Browning, and so the barrel was about five inches less and the body of the gun was made of Rolls-Royce 'Hiduminium' alloy. The mechanism was recoil-operated, using a system of locking very similar to the Degtyarev DP gun, two locking arms securing the bolt to the barrel extension until released when the striker was withdrawn. As might be imagined, the construction of the weapon was well up to Rolls-Royce standards.

The gun was tested in March 1941 and there were one or two minor malfunctions, but on the whole it was a sound design. The following month it was decided to rework the gun to fire the ·55-in cartridge used with the Boys anti-tank rifle, which would have given the gun a formidable performance. However, at that stage of the proceedings the Ministry of Aircraft Production stepped in and told Rolls-Royce that they would be better employed in bending their talents to the manufacture of aircraft engines, and that since the gun supply situation had taken a turn for the better the project was closed. So far as is known, only one specimen of the Rolls-Royce gun exists.

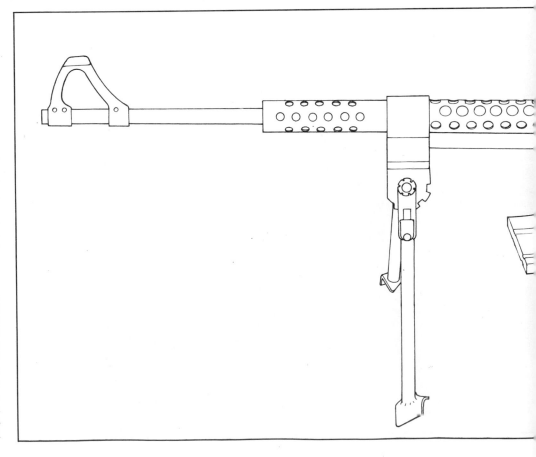

Stoner MMG
Experimental American 5.56-mm air-cooled machine-gun seen here in its medium-machine-gun role. It could also be converted to be carried as a light machine-gun with belted ammunition feeding from the right from a detachable box machine *Weight:* 10.2 lb *Rate of fire:* 650–850 rpm *Muzzle velocity:* 3250 fps

Over in Germany at that time there was a bottleneck in the supply of MG-34s. Even with all five factories at work there was still no sign of providing enough guns to meet the army's requirements, and Mauser were asked to develop a gun which was better suited to mass production. In order to start on the right foot, Mauser brought in a Dr Grunow of the Johannes Grossfuss Metall und Lackierwarenfabrik of Dobeln. Dr Grunow knew nothing about machine-guns, but he knew a lot about stamping out metal products in the cheapest and quickest way, and his advice, coupled with Mauser's expertise, made sure that the gun was designed with production facility well to the forefront, to suit stamping and pressing processes, with welding and riveting used for assembly.

The action of the MG-34 was changed so as to use a non-rotating bolt locking into a barrel extension by two rollers which were cammed outwards. Unless these rollers were out and the bolt securely locked, the firing pin could not pass through the bolt to strike the cap of the cartridge. On firing, the barrel and bolt recoiled back together until cam tracks in the gun body moved the rollers inwards to release the bolt. Movement of the bolt drove a feed arm mounted in the top cover of the gun which in turn operated pawls to feed the ammunition in from its belt.

Too fast for comfort

The new gun was designated the MG-42, and one of its unexpected results was the astonishing rate of fire of 1200 rpm, much higher than any other machine-gun of the time. As a result, the barrel had to be easily changed, and this was done by unlatching the breech end and swinging it out through a wide slot in the side of the barrel jacket until it could be slipped out. The barrel could be changed in less than five seconds. Another, less welcome, result of the rate of fire was that the gun vibrated

so much that it soon went off its point of aim and had a tendency to creep forward, away from the man holding it. But apart from that there was little complaint. It was extremely reliable in any conditions, very simple to operate and maintain, and proved popular with the soldiers. Over three-quarters of a million were made before the war ended.

It will be remembered that during the First World War the German air service called for a machine-gun with a high rate

of fire in order to improve chances of hitting in an air combat. Since the speed and manoeuvrability of aircraft had increased considerably in the intervening years, it is not surprising to find the same request being made once again during the course of the Second World War.

In view of Mauser's record with the MG-34, they had been given the task of developing a fast gun: their answer was the MG-81. This used the same basic mechanism as the MG-34 but had a recoil booster added

Goryunov SGT-43
This is the tank version of the Goryunov 7·62-mm M43, now known as the SGM and the current Russian medium machine-gun
Weight: 32 lb *Rate of fire:* 500—700 rpm
Muzzle velocity: 2620 fps

to the muzzle, which stepped up the rate of fire to about 1600 rpm. To give an even greater chance of hitting it was built as a two-barrelled gun mounted on a single gun body and carried in many Luftwaffe aircraft as an observer's free gun. Later it was adapted to pod assemblies which could be installed on Ju 88 night fighter conversions. Three double guns fitted in the pod, and aircraft could be armed with up to six such pods, giving a capability of discharging no less than 57,000 rounds a minute, a positively devastating weight of metal.

In 1943, with the Luftwaffe taking a less vital part in the war, many of these guns were taken away and, as single-barrelled weapons, given a bipod and butt for use as infantry machine-guns. While they were of some use, their extremely high rate of fire was largely wasted in this role and they were very difficult to control, spraying their ammunition in all directions.

In the USA only one machine-gun appeared to challenge the Browning, and this was the invention of Captain Melvin Johnson, USMC. Johnson had been designing firearms for several years: he had produced an automatic rifle which at one time was considered as a possible alternative to the Garand and which was adopted by the Dutch. He then produced a machine-gun which was tested by the US Marine Corps in 1941.

It operated on a combination of recoil and blowback, using recoil to unlock the bolt and blowback to complete the operation, and was unusual in being arranged so that it fired from a closed bolt at single shot and from an open bolt when firing automatic. In other words, when firing single shots the bolt was closed and locked and everything at rest when the cartridge was fired, while at automatic fire the bolt was held back until the trigger was pressed.

Dual advantage

The result of such a system is a more accurate fire at single shot, since the gunner's aim is not disturbed by the shift of balance as the bolt flies forward. On the other hand when firing automatic, and the gun is hot, the bolt stays in the rearmost position when the gun stops firing so that a cooling current of air can pass through the barrel, a measure which prevents loaded cartridges 'cooking-off'.

Johnson's gun was taken into service by the US Marines and by the US Army's Special Force in Italy, and was also ordered by the Dutch government for use in the Dutch East Indies. Unfortunately, before this order was even partly filled, the Indies had fallen to the Japanese, but the balance of the order went to swell the numbers supplied to the US forces. The Johnson was rather susceptible to dirt, but it had several ingenious features and it was revived some years after the war when a slightly modified version was put into limited production by the Israeli army as the 'Dror' machine-gun.

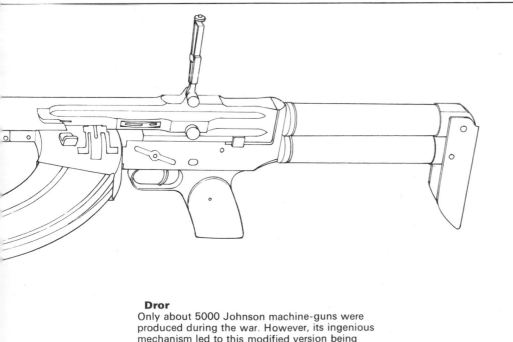

Dror
Only about 5000 Johnson machine-guns were produced during the war. However, its ingenious mechanism led to this modified version being produced in limited quantities by the Israeli army some years afterwards

POST-WAR DEVELOPMENTS: BACK TO BASICS

After the Second World War there was a pause in weapon development for a short time as the Western nations tried to get back to peace conditions and put military preparedness behind them. But it was soon obvious that the Communist Bloc had no intention of allowing the rest of the world to live in peaceful bliss, and within five years of the end of the war the weapon development staffs were at work once again.

One of the most interesting concepts to emerge from the war was a radical re-thinking of the basic infantry cartridge. For years this had been a full-sized powerful round firing a heavy bullet to ranges in the order of 2000 yards. During the war the Germans looked again at the fundamental requirements of an infantryman's weapon and came to the conclusion – supported by experience and statistics – that this was a gross waste of material and power. Rarely did the infantry soldier shoot at anything more than 400 yards away, and even then he didn't often hit it. So providing him with a weapon which would be accurate to 2000 yards was to no purpose. The Germans therefore developed a short cartridge which was perfectly satisfactory to ranges of about 750–800 yards, but which, being smaller and less powerful, allowed the rifle built for it to be smaller and lighter. It also allowed the soldier to carry more cartridges for a given weight.

Russian imitation

The Soviets saw the reasoning behind this, approved of it and began development of a similar cartridge together with a suitable automatic rifle. Once this was done, they turned to the manufacture of a machine-gun for the new cartridge. Work on this began, in fact, as early as 1943 when the new cartridge was in its first design stages. Since all the Soviet manufacturing capacity was hard at work on the standard DP and other guns needed at the front, development of the new design was at a low priority, but work was completed after the war and the new gun, known as the RPD, came into service in 1952.

As the 'D' implies, the gun was designed by Degtyarev, and was a modified version of his earlier DP gun, using flaps to lock the bolt but with a slightly different

arrangement to operate the flaps. The flimsy feed drum of the DP was discarded and a belt feed was substituted, the belt being carried in a feed box on the side of the gun. While the belt feed was an improvement in some respects, the fact remains that the basic design of the gun was based on an overhead feed, and making the gun lift the belt and drag it into the weapon added a load which it found difficult to sustain. Several minor changes were made in the gas system during the gun's life in order to try and generate more power and give more positive feed, but although the gun was a serviceable weapon and widely adopted by Communist nations it was nevertheless marginal in its efficiency.

The automatic rifle which had been developed for the new cartridge was the Kalashnikov AK-47, and experience with this weapon demonstrated that it had a better basic mechanism than did the DP or

FN MAG
Basically a development of the Browning Automatic Rifle with an MG-42 feed system, this Belgian 7·62-mm general purpose machine-gun is currently in service in several countries
Weight: 23·5 lb *Rate of fire:* 750–1000 rpm
Muzzle velocity: 2750 fps

The British L7A1 general purpose machine-gun version of the FN MAG, in the sustained fire role

RPD machine-guns. So to replace the RPD, the RPK was developed, based on the Kalashnikov rifle and little more than a heavier version of the rifle – indeed, the rifle bolt and piston are interchangeable with those of the machine-gun and the machine-gun will accept the rifle magazine should its own 75-round drum magazine not be available. Operation of the RPK is by gas, a piston rod being permanently attached to a bolt carrier. As the piston forces this carrier back, so a cam track within it rotates the bolt to unlock it and then withdraws it. The drum magazine clips on below the gun but, like the RPD before it, the RPK does not have a changeable barrel, which means that the gunner has to keep his rate of fire down in order to avoid overheating.

Another interesting Soviet machine-gun which appeared after the war, and which was designed around a cartridge rather than being designed purely as a gun, as it were, is the KPV heavy machine-gun. During the war the Soviets developed a very efficient anti-tank rifle in 14·5-mm calibre, and for this they manufactured an extremely powerful cartridge which had a 2-oz bullet and a muzzle velocity of 3200 fps. The rifle was obsolete by the time the war ended, such weapons being of little use against the wartime tanks, but the cartridge was too good to give up and the KPV was built to take advantage of it. The mechanism uses recoil assisted by a muzzle booster, and the whole gun is built in the simplest possible manner. The gun body is simply a steel tube, and welding and riveting are extensively used in assembly. It is an extremely robust weapon, though heavy, and is used as an anti-aircraft machine-gun and is sometimes found mounted on smaller armoured vehicles. Penetration is said to be about 1·5-in of armour at 100 yards range, and it is obviously a potent weapon against armoured personnel carriers.

Western development

In the Western nations the German short cartridge development had also caused some rethinking and much work went on to try and come up with something comparable. There was a good deal of political manoeuvring which tended to overshadow the basic ballistics of the question, and in the end the NATO nations agreed to accept a 7·62-mm cartridge which, although shorter

Kalashnikov PK

The heavy member of the Kalashnikov family (the others being the AKM assault rifle and the RPK light machine-gun), the 7·62-mm PK is gas-operated and has a cylindrical flash-hider with five longitudinal holes to help stability. An improved feed system and a facility for attaching an ammunition box are other new features
Weight: 21 lb *Rate of fire:* 750–1000 rpm
Muzzle velocity: 2800 fps

Degtyarev RPD

Produced after the war using the new M43 7·62-mm round, this light machine-gun was rather lacking in power, and was superseded in Russian service by the RPK. Shown here with breech open *Weight:* 15·5 lb *Rate of fire:* 650–750 rpm *Muzzle velocity:* 2400 fps

than the general run of wartime rifle cartridges, was by no means as short as the German or Soviet designs. With this settled, work began on finding suitable machine-guns, and most nations agreed that the German idea of a general purpose machine-gun was a good target to aim at. In Britain the first solution was a somewhat heavier

Bren gun, altered to belt feed, but this was not particularly successful and eventually it was decided to adopt a Belgian design, the Fabrique Nationale's 'MAG' (*Mitrailleur à Gaz*, or gas-operated machine-gun).

It will be recalled that John Browning went to FN in the early years of the century for the development of many of his designs, and the company had been working on his designs ever since. So it is hardly surprising to find that the MAG uses the same basic mechanism as the Browning Automatic Rifle, though adapting the bolt locking system so that the bolt moves down to lock instead of up. This change was necessary since the MAG was designed to feed from a belt, and the feed mechanism was copied

from the German MG-42, which demanded that a stud in the top of the bolt drive the feed linkage.

Like all FN products, the MAG was well thought out and well engineered, and it was an immediate success. It is currently used by 20 countries as their standard machine-gun and is doubtless to be found in smaller numbers in many others.

At the close of the war the US Army had a variety of Browning guns in service. The medium gun was either the water-cooled M1917 or the air-cooled M2, and the squad light machine-gun was either the M1919A6 – which was nothing more than an air-cooled M2 with a butt and bipod – or the Automatic Rifle. In addition there were various sub-models, and various tank and anti-aircraft models in ·30 and ·50 calibre. While the Browning was undoubtedly a splendid gun, this profusion of models was getting out of hand, and before the war had ended, plans were laid for clearing them away and producing a completely new General Purpose model.

At one stage there was a possibility that the US might have gone into production

with a copy of the German MG-42, as they were so impressed with it. A company was given some MG-42s and a contract to develop a copy as the US T24 machine-gun. After about a year's work two guns were built but their test was a fiasco. What started out as a 'ten thousand round endurance test'

M60
The American general purpose machine-gun, this 7·62-mm weapon was developed from the wartime German MG-42 and FG-42. It replaced the BAR and the water-cooled Browning
Weight: 23 lb *Rate of fire:* 600 rpm
Muzzle velocity: 2800 fps

came to a stop after just over 1000 rounds had been fired with 50 stoppages. Investigation showed that a draughtsman had made a small error in dimensioning the gun, with the result that the body was a quarter of an inch too short, leading in turn to various malfunctions. The amount of redesign needed to sort this out was considered to be not worthwhile, and the project was cancelled.

After that inauspicious start several other projects were initiated, but it was not until the acceptance of the 7·62-mm NATO cartridge that serious work could begin. Once the cartridge was agreed, the M60 machine-gun took shape. Much of the design was taken from German originals. The gas piston and rotating bolt came from the Parachutist Automatic Rifle, and the belt feed system from the MG-42. The only really novel feature was the use of what is called a 'constant energy' gas regulator in the gas system. Most machine-guns using gas pistons simply allow the gas to go into the port in the barrel and push on the piston, exhausting the gas once the piston has moved off. Should the gun get dirty, and thus require more power to operate it, the gunner can usually adjust the gas port to deliver more gas and thus get a more powerful impulse to drive the gun.

The M60, on the other hand, delivers its gas into a hollow piston through holes in the side. As soon as the piston moves, driving the gun operating rod, the holes in it move away from the gas port in the barrel and the supply of gas is stopped. The piston thus receives a sharp kick to drive the gun instead of a more sustained push.

In theory this should be sufficient, since the piston will not move until it has enough energy to overcome the stiffness of the gun mechanism, so that if there is more resistance than usual then more gas will enter the piston. In practice, though, the reserve of power just isn't there. Another snag is that it is perfectly possible to put the piston into the cylinder back-to-front so that the holes do not line up, and the gun will then fire one shot and stop.

On the credit side, the M60 was designed with production in mind and it makes considerable use of stampings and pressings in its assembly. The barrel can be changed, though not very quickly and it has no handle, so that the gunner has to be provided with an asbestos glove to grip the hot barrel. One way and another, one is forced to the conclusion that the M60 isn't

Heckler & Koch HK21
This commercially produced weapon is currently being evaluated by several armies. It is a delayed blowback gun using the same system, and many components, as the G3 rifle. It is available chambered for 7·62-mm NATO, 7·62 × 39 Soviet or 5·56-mm (·223-in) cartridges, and can be belt- or magazine-fed *Weight:* 17·6 lb *Rate of fire:* 900 rpm *Muzzle velocity:* 2624 fps (Data for 7·62-mm NATO version)

AAT 52
The French *Arme Automatique Transformable* was produced as a GPMG in the early 1950s. Cheap production techniques allied to a powerful 7·5-mm cartridge make it somewhat prone to jamming *Weight:* 24 lb *Rate of fire:* 600 rpm *Muzzle velocity:* 2700 fps

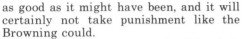

Vulcan M61
The General Electric 20-mm aircraft cannon uses the electric-powered Gatling principle
Weight: 255 lb *Rate of fire:* 6000 rpm
Muzzle velocity: 3450 fps

as good as it might have been, and it will certainly not take punishment like the Browning could.

The French army stayed with their Chatellerault for several years after the war, but they too began looking to a General Purpose gun in the early 1950s and produced the AAT 52, or *Arme Automatique Transformable*. This was designed with simplicity and cheapness in mind, the body, for example, being two steel pressings welded together.

The action is rather unusual for such a powerful weapon, being a delayed blowback. The system closely resembles that used with the Hungarian Danuvia submachine-gun of 1939, a two-piece bolt with a lever in between the two sections which engages in a recess in the gun body. When the gun fires, the light bolt head recoils, but has to rotate the lever out of engagement with its recess before the movement can be transmitted to the heavier bolt body and allow the whole unit to recoil. As is usual with blowback guns this leads to problems in extraction, and the AAT 52 has the chamber fluted so as to float the case on gas and ease extraction. Nevertheless, the ejected cases frequently show signs of bulging, indicating that pressure is still very high when the case begins to leave the breech. The AAT still uses the 7·5-mm cartridge developed in 1929, but there is also another model which is chambered for the 7·62-mm NATO round.

The 'Salvo' studies
In 1952 the United States Army set up a research project called 'Salvo' in order to do some fundamental research into infantry fire. Close study of statistics of casualties in action, post-combat analyses and interviews with hundreds of soldiers who had some combat experience led the researchers to some remarkable conclusions. In the first place it seemed that most casualties from rifle fire were due to sheer bad luck, in that the majority of them were the result of chance shots. Secondly, the ratio of ammunition expended to casualties produced was astronomical. Thirdly, many men admitted that in the heat of action they rarely took pains over aiming their rifle or machine-gun, but merely pointed it in the right direction and pulled the trigger. All this led to the question, 'Is the powerful and long range rifle any use at all?' – which, it will be remembered, is much the same

question as the Germans had asked in 1941.

The result of this research was a programme to develop smaller-calibre weapons, as well as weapons capable of firing multi-shot ammunition, items which

do not come into our sphere of interest. But one of the products of the programme was the 5·56-mm (·223-in) cartridge, which was first put to use in the well-known Armalite series of rifles. Soon the 5·56-mm cartridge began to assume an important role. It was widely used in Vietnam, and eventually the US Army announced that their forces in Europe would henceforth be equipped with 5·56-mm weapons. This reduced faith in the 7·62-mm NATO cartridge, and since this announcement in 1970 there has been considerable activity in developing weapons to take the 5·56-mm cartridge.

Automatic rifles were the first to be developed, and after that the question of machine-guns arose. At first there was a feeling that the 5·56-mm was no good in a

GE Six-Pak
This lightweight 5.56-mm (.223-in) version of the 7.62-mm Minigun may well enter service as a high-speed ground gun *Weight:* 26 lb (gun only) *Rate of fire:* 10,000 rpm max
Muzzle velocity: 3300 fps

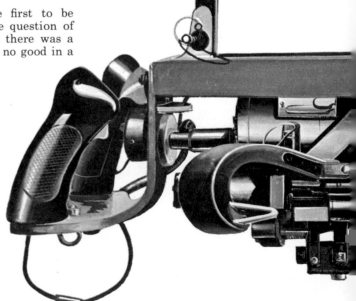

M134 Minigun
The 7·62-mm electrically-driven Minigun on a ground pedestal mounting. Its voracious consumption of ammunition makes it rather impractical as a ground gun *Weight:* 45·5 lb (gun only) *Rate of fire:* 6000 rpm *Muzzle velocity:* 2800 fps

machine-gun, since it did not have the long-ranging ability for sustained barrage and covering fire which was one of the traditional roles of the machine-gun. But the 'Salvo' studies were as valid for machine-guns as they were for rifles, and the long-range ability became less and less important. Improvements in the design of the 5·56-mm bullet, allied with research into

the best twist of rifling, also gave improvements in the bullet's range, until in the end the maximum range of the bullet and the minimum range acceptable to the traditional machine-gunners more or less coincided.

Research continues on a large scale into machine-guns in 5·56-mm and even smaller calibres – although the Americans, having

by any nation, but there are signs that the first 5·56-mm machine-gun might well enter service shortly.

In order to bring this study of the machine-gun to a close, it would be fitting to complete the circle and end up almost where we began – with the Gatling gun.

In 1944 the US Air Force asked for a fast-firing machine-gun, much the same sort of request which we have already seen made in Germany, and during the early days of research somebody remembered that Gatling had fitted an electric motor to a gun to get a high rate of fire. To see whether there was anything in the idea, a Gatling was borrowed from a museum and fitted with an electric motor, whereupon it delivered 5000 rounds per minute. This was obviously the way to go, and the Armaments Division of the General Electric company were given a contract under the project name of 'Vulcan', the Greek god of fire.

Vulcans and Miniguns

By 1949 a prototype gun of ·60-in calibre was ready for test, and this delivered 6000 rpm from a six-barrelled unit driven electrically. Development continued, changing the calibre to 20-mm so that explosive shells could be fired, and in 1956 the 20-mm M61 Vulcan gun entered service. A 30-mm model then followed, and both these heavy-weights became standard US Air Force armament. Then in the early 1960s the designers turned their attention to the smaller calibres and developed 7·62-mm and 5·56-mm 'Minigun' versions.

The M134 7·62-mm Minigun uses six barrels driven by a 28-volt electric motor. An electronic control system allows selection of any two rates of fire between 400 rpm minimum and 6000 rpm maximum. While it is possible to mount the gun on a form of ground stand, the need for ammunition troughs to cope with the gun's enormous appetite, the provision of batteries and the electronic gear all mean that as a ground weapon it is scarcely practical. But mounted in a vehicle as an anti-aircraft weapon, or mounted in a helicopter for ground attack, the minigun can deliver a devastating stream of fire which is so concentrated that it can chop its way through undergrowth or light buildings to get at the men trying to take cover.

The 5·56-mm version is known as the 'GE Six-Pak' and is currently being examined by the US Army and Air Force. Due to its smaller size (the whole gun and power unit, with 1000 rounds of ammunition, weighs only 85 lb) this is feasible as a ground machine-gun. With six barrels it delivers 4000 rounds per minute, and there is every prospect that the Six-Pak will eventually enter service. The Gatling gun has come a long way in 110 years.

set everybody on their ears by embracing the 5·56-mm cartridge, are now talking about dropping it in favour of a new 6·0-mm design. In Germany, the Heckler & Koch company have produced 5·56-mm models, while in the USA there is the Colt CMG-2, the Foote MG-69 and the Stoner 63A all perfected and undergoing various tests. At the time of writing, none has been adopted

MACHINE-GUN DATA TABLE

GUN	CALIBRE	LENGTH INS	BARREL LENGTH INS	WEIGHT LBS	FEED	RATE OF FIRE RDS/MIN	MUZZLE VELOCITY FT/SEC
AUSTRIA							
Schwarzlose M07/12	8mm	42	20.75	44	250 Belt	400	2050
BELGIUM							
FN MAG	7.62mm	49.2	21.5	22.25	Link Belt	850	2800
CZECHOSLOVAKIA							
ZB26	7.92mm	45.75	26.5	21.3	30 Box	500	2500
DENMARK							
Madsen M1903	.303in	45	23	20	40 Box	450	2350
FRANCE							
Hotchkiss Puteaux	8mm	—	—	54	23 Strip	650	230
Hotchkiss St Etienne	8mm	46.5	28	56.75	30 Strip	400–500	2300
Hotchkiss Model 1914	8mm	50	30.5	52	30 Strip	600	2380
Hotchkiss FM1922	6.5mm	44.1	23.6	21.4	250 Belt	650	—
Chauchat M1915	8mm	45	18.5	20	20 Box	250	2300
Chatellerenault M1924	7.5mm	42.6	19.7	20.25	25 Box	500	2700
AAT 52	7.62mm	39	19.3	21.75	50 Belt	700	2700
GERMANY							
Bergmann M1910	7.92mm	—	—	36	200 Belt	550	2952
Bergmann M1915nA	7.92mm	44.13	28.5	28.5	200 Belt	500	2925
Dreyse MG-13	7.92mm	—	—	37.5	200 Belt	550–600	2952
Gast M1918	7.92mm	54.72	28.35	60	180 Drum	1800	2900
Heckler & Koch HK21	7.62mm	40	17.7	14.8	50 Belt	750	2625
Mauser MG-34	7.92mm	48	24.75	26.9	50 Belt	800–900	2480

US Marines on guard with an M60 machine-gun on the Khe Sanh perimeter, Vietnam in March 1968

GUN	CALIBRE	LENGTH INS	BARREL LENGTH INS	WEIGHT LBS	FEED	RATE OF FIRE RDS/MIN	MUZZLE VELOCITY FT/SEC
Mauser MG-42	7.92mm	48	21	25.8	50 Belt	1200	2480
Mauser MG-81	7.92mm	37	18.6	14	250 Belt	1250	2750
Maxim 1908	7.92mm	46.25	28.3	58.3	250 Belt	300–450	2925
Maxim '08/15	7.92mm	57	28.3	39	250 Belt	450	2925
Rheinmetall MG-15	7.92mm	52.5	23.5	28	75 Drum	850	2480
Rheinmetall MG-3	7.62mm	48.2	22.2	24.4	Belt	850	2690
Solothurn MG-30	7.92mm	46.25	23.5	17	25 Box	800	2500

GREAT BRITAIN

GUN	CALIBRE	LENGTH INS	BARREL LENGTH INS	WEIGHT LBS	FEED	RATE OF FIRE RDS/MIN	MUZZLE VELOCITY FT/SEC
Beardmore-Farquhar	.303in	50	26	16.25	77 Drum	450–500	2427
Besa Mk1	7.92mm	43.5	29	47	225 Belt	450–500	2700
Besal	.303in	46.63	22	21.5	30 Box	600	2450
Bren Mk1	.303in	45.25	25	22.3	30 Box	500	2400
Lewis gun .303 Mk1	.303in	50.5	26.25	26	97 Drum	550	2450
Maxim Model 1884	.303in	46.5	28.25	40	250 Belt	600	2750
Maxim .303	.303in	46.5	28.5	40	250 Belt	600	2440
Vickers .303 Mk1	.303in	45.5	28.5	40	250 Belt	450	2450
Vickers-Berthier M3	.303in	46.5	23.5	22	30 Box	600	2450

ISRAEL

GUN	CALIBRE	LENGTH INS	BARREL LENGTH INS	WEIGHT LBS	FEED	RATE OF FIRE RDS/MIN	MUZZLE VELOCITY FT/SEC
Dror	7.92mm	42.5	22	14.75	20 Box	300–900	2800

ITALY

GUN	CALIBRE	LENGTH INS	BARREL LENGTH INS	WEIGHT LBS	FEED	RATE OF FIRE RDS/MIN	MUZZLE VELOCITY FT/SEC
Breda M1930	6.5mm	48.5	20.5	22.75	20 Box	450–500	2063
Breda M1937	8mm	50	26.75	43	20 Strip	450	2600
Breda Safat M1935	7.7mm	–	–	27	Belt	800	2400
Fiat M1935	8mm	–	26	40	Belt	500	2600
Fiat Revelli M1914	6.5mm	46.5	25.75	37.5	50 Box	400	2100
Perino M1908	7.7mm	–	–	50	25 Strip	600	2400
Vilar Perosa	9mm	21.1	12.6	18	30 Box	800	1200

JAPAN

GUN	CALIBRE	LENGTH INS	BARREL LENGTH INS	WEIGHT LBS	FEED	RATE OF FIRE RDS/MIN	MUZZLE VELOCITY FT/SEC
Taisho 11 Model	6.5mm	43.5	19	22.5	30 Hopper	500	2300
Taisho 3	6.5mm	45.5	29.5	62	30 Strip	400	2400
Type 92	7.7mm	45.5	27.5	122	30 Strip	450	2400
Type 96	6.5mm	41.5	21.7	20	30 Box	550	2400
Type 99	7.7mm	46.5	21.5	23	30 Box	850	2350

SOVIET UNION

GUN	CALIBRE	LENGTH INS	BARREL LENGTH INS	WEIGHT LBS	FEED	RATE OF FIRE RDS/MIN	MUZZLE VELOCITY FT/SEC
Degtyarev DP	7.62mm	50.8	23.8	20.5	47 Drum	500–600	2760
Degtyarev DShK	12.7mm	62.5	42	78.5	50 Belt	550	2825
Degtyarev RPD	7.62mm	41	20.5	15.4	100 Belt	700	2410
Goryunov SG-43	7.62mm	44.1	28.3	30.25	Belt	600	2440
Kalashnikov RPK	7.62mm	41	23.2	10.5	75 Drum	600	2400
KPV	14.5mm	78.8	53.1	108	Belt	600	3250
Maxim M1910	7.62mm	43.6	28.4	52.5	250 Belt	520–580	2830

UNITED STATES

GUN	CALIBRE	LENGTH INS	BARREL LENGTH INS	WEIGHT LBS	FEED	RATE OF FIRE RDS/MIN	MUZZLE VELOCITY FT/SEC
Browning M1917 A1	.30in	38.5	24	32.8	250 Belt	500	2800
Browning Automatic Rifle M1918 A2	.30in	47.8	24.07	19.4	20 Box	500–600	2650
Browning .30 M2	.30in	39.9	23.9	23	250 Belt	1200	2800
Browning .50 M2	.50in	65.1	45	84	110 Belt	500	2950
Browning .30 M1919 A4	.30in	41	24	31	250 Belt	550	2800
Colt CMG-2	5.56mm	41.9	–	13	Belt	650	3250
Colt M1895	7.65mm	47.25	28.35	37	300 Belt	400–500	–
GE Six-Pak	5.56mm	41	27	33	Link Belt	10000	3250
Johnson M1941	.30in	42	22	14.3	20 Box	300–900	2800
M60	7.62mm	43.75	25.5	23	Link Belt	600	2800
M61 Vulcan	20mm	73.8	–	264	Belt	6600	3450
M134 Minigun	7.62mm	31.5	22	67.0	Belt	6000	2850
Marlin	.30in	40	28	22.5	250 Belt	660	2800
Maxim M1904	.30in	–	–	40	250 Belt	600	2750

DELIVERING A HAIL OF FIRE

A US Army despatch-rider shows the world the
business-end of his Thompson submachine-gun
from behind the shelter of his Harley-Davidson
motorcycle

Although sometimes referred to derisively as a 'gangster gun', the submachine-gun was a military development. It was born during the First World War, came through a precarious adolescence between the wars, and finally reached maturity during the Second World War. In the years which followed its influence has spread and it can now be found in every military armoury. However, there are signs that its importance is declining, and informed opinion is that it is likely to vanish from military service by 1990.

In order to follow the history of the submachine-gun it is first necessary to define just what a submachine-gun is. Even the title has changed over the years; many continental nations referred to the weapon as a 'machine-pistol', others as a 'machine-carbine'. While both these expressions have some validity, they tend to be confusing, since there are other weapons which can be described in the same way. A 'machine-pistol' can also mean an ordinary self-loading ('automatic') pistol converted to fire in the full-automatic mode and generally fitted with some sort of shoulder-stock. This is not a particularly efficient weapon and cannot be considered in the same class as the 'proper' submachine-gun. The term 'machine-carbine' can also be used to cover weapons which are purely lightweight self-loading rifles with or without an automatic fire capability, though this type of weapon tends to attract the term 'assault-rifle'.

The submachine-gun, on the other hand, has certain definite and recognisable features. Firstly, it normally fires a pistol cartridge. Secondly it is a magazine-fed automatic weapon, that is one which will continue to fire while the trigger remains pressed and there is a supply of ammunition in the magazine – although this does not preclude the fitting of some sort of selector mechanism to allow the firing of single shots for each pressure on the trigger. Thirdly, it is meant to be fired two-handed, either from the hip or from the shoulder. Any weapon which satisfies these three requirements can fairly be called a submachine-gun.

Mass Armies

With a few notable exceptions submachine-guns have been produced with the intention of providing overwhelming fire-power for mass armies in the shortest possible time. This mass-production demand led to the logical request that the mechanism be simple and easily made, robust and resistant to the dirt and damage liable to be met on the battlefield. Consequently, the system of operation generally selected is that known as the 'blow-back' or 'spent case projection' system. This system utilises the gas pressure generated within the cartridge case at the instant of firing to push the bullet through the barrel and, at the same time, exerts a rearward pressure on the breech-block, or bolt, which is supporting the cartridge case in the breech. The difference in mass between the bullet and the breech-block means that the light bullet passes up the barrel and leaves the muzzle before the breech-block has managed to overcome its own inertia. The gas pressure then exhausts through the barrel behind the bullet and the pressure within the breech drops to a level at which it is safe to begin extracting the empty cartridge case. By this time the breech-block has begun to move and there is sufficient residual pressure to operate the weapon. Once inertia is overcome, the

impulse given to the base of the cartridge and the block takes effect, and the block is driven backwards against the pressure of a spring. An extractor in the block withdraws the spent case and ejects it, the recoiling block being stopped by the compression of its spring. The spring then re-asserts itself and pushes the block back to the gun breech, stripping a fresh cartridge from the magazine on the way and feeding it into the chamber. With the round chambered, the striker hits the cap and the cartridge explodes, to begin the cycle all over again.

That is the simple blow-back action, used in hundreds of small-calibre lightweight pocket pistols. But the submachine-gun is usually chambered for one of the more powerful pistol cartridges, cartridges which demand a locked breech system of operation when used in a pistol. The considerable difference in the mass of the bullet and the mass of a submachine-gun breech-block is in favour of using such a cartridge. However, it then becomes necessary to take extra precautions to ensure that the breech supports the cartridge case for long enough to allow the pressure to drop to a safe level.

The necessary safety is most usually obtained by making use of a principle known variously as 'inertia locking' or 'differential locking'. The cycle of operation is so arranged that the charge in the cartridge is fired a fraction of a second before the breech-block reaches its extreme forward position, so that as the cartridge fires the breech-block is actually moving forward, carrying the cartridge with it. This means that the explosion pressure must first of all arrest the forward motion of the block before it can overcome the block's inertia and start it moving backwards. The infinitesimal delay generated by this system is just enough to provide the desired level of safety and, in addition, the recoil force on the firer is reduced by virtue of the absorption of recoil in the process of reversing the movement of the block. The actual 'premature' firing of the cartridge is usually done by making the chamber a tight fit around the case, so that as the case is chambered by the forward movement of the bolt, it puts up sufficient resistance when almost fully home to allow the striker to hit the cap with a force powerful enough to fire it. Other systems have been used to achieve the same result, and these will be explained where they occur in particular guns, but this method of 'inertia locking' is by far the most common.

Some designers have preferred to make use of systems of operation which are more positive in their checking of the breech-block movement, though a fully-locked breech on a submachine-gun is something of a rarity.

The Basic Submachine-Gun

In order to explain some of the terms used in the body of the book, it would be as well to consider here a typical and simple submachine-gun and identify the parts and method of operation.

The gun will consist basically of a **Receiver**, the body of the gun which carries all the working parts; the **Barrel**, which is formed into the **Chamber** at its rear end; and the **Stock** or **Butt** which enables the firer to hold it. In addition there may be one or more **Pistol Grips** to allow more convenient holding; there will also be a **Magazine Housing** forming part of the receiver and into which the **Magazine** is inserted before firing. The magazine may be

a **Drum** type in which the cartridges are arranged in a spiral path and fed to the **Magazine Lips** by a spring drive of some sort; or it may be a **Box Magazine** in which the cartridges are held in a straight line and similarly fed to the lips by spring power. In some weapons the magazine is placed on top of the gun, feeding downwards by force of gravity assisted by a light spring; others feed from the side, others from underneath. Some magazines have the cartridges in a single row, some in a double column; generally speaking the latter type are more easy to fill and more reliable in operation. Some types of magazine demand a special tool to fill them, and this is not a particularly good feature, since these inevitably get lost just when they are needed.

The **Sights** are usually fairly simple types of aperture at the rear and blade at the front, fixed for operation at a range of about 100 yards, though in the early days of the submachine-gun it was common to find adjustable backsights graduated to ranges of 1000 yards or more; since those days the limitations of the weapons have been better appreciated, and such optimistic devices are rarely seen today. The **Stock** may be of wood or of plastic material, or even of light metal, and capable of being folded up in some way or another to make the weapon easier to stow away in vehicles and handier to use in confined spaces, though firing a submachine-gun without having the stock tucked into the shoulder or trapped beneath the arm is a somewhat inaccurate exercise and only recommended in an emergency.

The mechanism is usually designed so that the gun fires from an **Open Bolt**. This means that in order to fire the **Bolt** is pulled back by a **Cocking Lever** of some sort until it is held back, against the power of the **Bolt Return Spring**, by a **Sear** which is part of the **Firing Mechanism** and controlled by the **Trigger**. A **Safety Catch** of some sort may be fitted, and also a **Fire Selector** which allows the firer to choose either single shots or automatic fire. On more modern designs there may be an additional **Grip Safety** which prevents the weapon from firing unless it is properly held in a firing attitude and thus it cannot inadvertently fire if dropped or mishandled.

To fire the gun the trigger is pressed, which withdraws the sear and allows the bolt to run forward propelled by its spring. As the bolt passes the magazine lips, so it strikes the edge of the topmost cartridge and forces it forward, out of the magazine, and pushes it into the **Chamber**, the **Extractor** on the bolt snapping over the rim of the cartridge during this movement. When the cartridge is firmly in the chamber the **Firing Pin** or **Striker** hits the cap and explodes the propellant charge, driving the bullet through the barrel and exerting rearward pressure on the case and through it on to the face of the bolt. This drives the bolt back against the pressure of the return spring; the extractor pulls the empty cartridge case from the chamber and holds on to it until the rearward movement brings the case up against an **Ejector**, which flings the empty case out through the **Ejection Port** in the side of the receiver.

When the bolt has compressed the return spring to a sufficient degree to halt the rearward movement, it stops, and then begins to travel forward again. If the trigger is still pressed and the selector set for automatic firing, the bolt will travel straight forward, collect a fresh round, chamber it, fire it, and go through the whole sequence again, repeating this as long as there are cartridges in the magazine and the trigger is held down. But if the trigger has been released, or if the selector is set for firing single shots, then the sear will rise into the path of the bolt and hold it in the rearward position, ready to be released when the trigger is next pressed.

Since the bolt is always in this rearward position when the weapon is ready to fire, the gun is said to fire from an **Open Bolt**. This is a valuable safety factor, since the high rate of fire of a submachine-gun, together with the short barrel, means that the barrel soon reaches a very high temperature. If the gun were not firing from an open bolt but from a **Closed Bolt**, this would mean that whenever the gun was prepared for firing, the bolt would be closed with a cartridge in the chamber, but with the firing pin prevented from striking the cap until the trigger was actually pressed. If the gun had already been fired, this would mean that a live cartridge would have been loaded into a hot chamber. The chances are that the temperature would be so high that within a few seconds the heat of the chamber and barrel would be conducted through the thin brass of the cartridge case to the propellant powder inside. The round would then 'Cook Off', or fire by induced heat, generally to the surprise of the man holding the gun and the dismay of some poor innocent bystander who collects the bullet through his leg. The advantage of the open bolt is, therefore, that while the bolt is held back a cooling current of air can pass down the barrel, and the interior of the gun can also cool down.

There is a disadvantage, however. Firing from an open bolt means that when the trigger is pressed there is an appreciable pause while the bolt goes forward, chambers the round and fires it. There is also a considerable shift in the balance of the gun as the mass of the bolt moves forward, and thus the possibility of accurately firing the first shot is reduced. The sight picture and the point of aim will wander while the bolt is moving, due to both the delay and the shift in balance. As a rule, the designer has to make up his mind what object he has in view – either an accurate first-shot weapon, in which case he must go for the closed bolt and make some provision for cooling the barrel and lowering the risk of a cook-off – or a 'hosepipe' weapon, in which results are achieved by sheer volume of fire and accurate first-round accuracy is forgotten. It is, in fact, possible to have the best of both worlds and devise a mechanism which fires single shots from a closed bolt and automatic fire from an open bolt, though this demands complicated engineering.

These, then, are the basics. How they have been achieved in various models, how different designers have solved the problems, and how other refinements have been introduced from time to time, will be dealt with in the pages that follow. The basic features however remain the same. Somehow you have to get the cartridge into the gun, fire it, utilise the energy to reload and recock the weapon, continue to do this as long as required, and do it in as reliable and convenient a manner as can be devised. On the face of it, it seems simple enough. But as the following pages will show, there are more ways of killing a cat than choking it with cream.

Foresight

Jacket

Barrel

Bolt

Butt folded forward

Firing Pin

Sear

Trigger

EXTRACTING

Sterling Machine-Carbine 9-mm
The L2A3 is the current service version of the original Patchett prototype. The L2A1 entered service in 1953 and despite minor modifications, today's weapon is substantially the same. Made entirely from steel and plastic, the Sterling has a folding stock and side-feeding box magazine. Although expensively made to fine tolerances, the weapon is extremely durable and reliable. A silenced version, intended to replace the Mk 6 Sten is known as the L34A1 *Weight:* 7 lb 9 oz *Rate of fire:* 550 rpm *Muzzle velocity:* 1250 fps

Cocking Handle

Return Spring

Backsight

Ejection Port

Folding Butt

Magazine

Ejector

Chamber

Extractor

LOADING

TRENCH-BROOMS AND BULLET-SQUIRTERS

There are two opinions about the weapon which can lay claim to being the first submachine-gun; the first weapon to fall inside our quoted definition was the Vilar Perosa machine-gun, developed in Italy in late 1915. It was designed by A B Revelli, a noted Italian weapon designer, and took its name from being first made in the factory of Officine Vilar Perosa in the Italian town of the same name. Two other Italian factories also made this gun, and some were made in Canada for a short time in 1917–18.

However, the Vilar Perosa was far from being a submachine-gun in appearance, whatever it may have been mechanically. It consisted of two small machine-guns mounted side-by-side, fitted with overhead magazines, and fired by spade grips in the manner of a heavy machine-gun. Some had bipods, but most had a form of central pivot mounting and could be attached to a variety of mounts for use on ships, vehicles or tripods. Others were made with the barrels linked by a geared system which allowed them to be set at different angles to each other so as to allow the bullets to converge at some definite distance from the muzzles; these were used in aircraft in order to concentrate the fire at a fixed range.

The mechanism was of the blow-back type, but with an element of delay introduced, and with the usual differential locking incorporated. The bolt was formed with a lug which travelled in a groove in the receiver and which forced the bolt to rotate 15° as it closed up to the breech. At the same time the striker, which had a cam riding in

a groove in the bolt, was driven by this rotation on to the cartridge cap, firing the round just before the closing action was completed. The recoil force then had to 'unwind' the bolt and striker in their cam paths before they could recoil, and this gave a slight delay to the bolt opening action as an additional safety measure.

The magazines were fed by gravity, with spring assistance, and they were notable for being slotted at the rear edge so that the firer could, at any time, give a quick glance glance to see how many rounds were left. While this was excellent in theory, it was less good in practice since the slots allowed dirt to enter the magazine and upset the feeding. The ammunition used was a pistol round, the 9-mm Glisenti cartridge.

However, the tactical application of the Vilar Perosa was far from being that of a submachine-gun; it was actually intended as a light machine-gun for infantry support. This arose from the fact that the Italian Army had difficulties with their machine-guns, largely owing to the peculiar systems they chose to adopt and the somewhat peculiar small-calibre rifle cartridge they used. Their standard First World War machine-gun was the Revelli, a heavy and not particularly reliable weapon which was far from ideal in the mountain warfare conditions which the Italians encountered on most of their front with the Austrians. The lightweight Vilar Perosa was therefore intended as the mountain troop machine-gun, mounted on a bipod or tripod and sometimes even with a heavy steel shield.

However, due to the relatively weak pistol round, it was not a conspicuous success in this role, since its range was limited, and it eventually found its niche when slung from the shoulders of a walking soldier by means of a strap and supporting tray. In this way he could hold the spade grips at waist level and fire the guns as he advanced. The rate of fire was astronomical – 3000 rounds a minute when both barrels were firing – and this was unfortunate, since the magazines only held 20 rounds for each barrel and they emptied very quickly. It was normal to fire only one barrel at a time in order to conserve ammunition, and the operator carried some 600 rounds, ready loaded in magazines, but magazine changes at frequent intervals was still quite a performance.

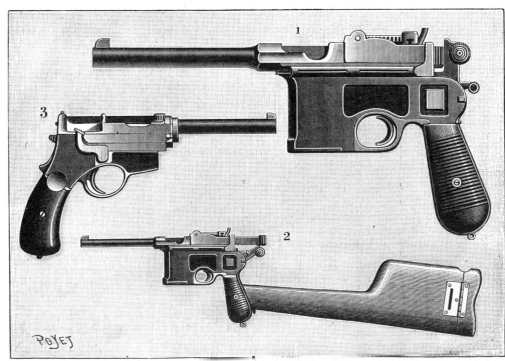

The Mauser and Mannlicher pistols of 1898 were also available with a stock doubling up as a holster

Luger Model 08/14 9-mm Parabellum
The long-barrelled 1914 Model of the famous
Navy 08 Parabellum pistol was issued in 1917
with a stock and a 32-round spring operated
'snail' magazine designed by the Austro-
Hungarians Tatarek and von Benko who had
patented the device in 1911. However impressive
it looked the combination was cumbersome and
prone to jamming *Weight:* (pistol only) 2 lb 5 oz
Muzzle velocity: 1250 fps

This, then, is the weapon generally considered to be the grandfather of the submachine-gun. But it will be clear from the
description that while it may qualify on
mechanical grounds, it certainly bears little
resemblance to the weapons which came
after it. The second contender for the
pioneer's title, and the gun which, in my
opinion, was the first real submachine-gun,
was the Bergmann *Musquete* or *Kugelspritz*
(Bullet-squirter) which reached the German
Army early in 1918.

Once again, the development of this
weapon was spurred by the short-comings
in the array of armament available, but it
was given an extra filip by the emergence of
fresh tactical doctrines at the crucial
moment. The standard German machine-

gun was the Maxim 08, another heavy water-
cooled weapon similar to the British Vickers
and the Italian Revelli, though a good deal
more reliable than the latter. In an attempt
to make the Maxim into a more handy
weapon for use by assault-troops rather
than an emplaced weapon, it was lightened
to become the Model '08/15. This was a very
good weapon indeed, but it was hardly a
light machine-gun – it weighed 31 lbs, and
with the weight penalty and all the other
impedimenta considered necessary in those
days, it took a fairly tough soldier to carry
one for any length of time.

In an effort to break the stalemate on the
Western Front, the German Army had
begun to experiment with new tactics first
suggested by General von Hutier and em-

ployed by him on the Eastern Front. This
involved making up parties of *Stosstruppen*
(Storm Troops), lightly equipped and well
armed, who could advance in small bunches
and infiltrate around obstacles under cover
of smoke and gas bombardments, concen-
trating on carving a path for the reinforcing
infantry to follow, instead of merely advanc-
ing in an extended line like so many
automata, as had been the disastrous military orthodoxy until then. Such parties
needed overwhelming firepower in order to
deal quickly with anything in their path,
and they did not want to be burdened
with the '08/15. These two lines of thought
– the demand for a lighter machine-gun
and the demand for a highly portable form
of fire-power – came together with the

development of the Bergmann *Musquete*.

The Bergmann weapon – which was later known by the more official title of the Maschinen Pistole 1918 or MP-18 – was designed by Hugo Schmeisser, a man who was the son of a foremost firearms designer and who was to become even more famous in his own right in years to come. The construction was quite simple – a tubular receiver carried a heavy bolt and a return spring which acted through the medium of the firing pin holder to deliver pressure to the bolt. The barrel was enclosed inside a perforated jacket-cum-handguard, and the metal components rested in a heavy wooden stock. The barrel and receiver were hinged to the front of the stock and were retained in place by a simple catch at the rear end. Operation of this catch allowed the entire gun unit to be swung up, after which a cap at the rear of the receiver was pressed in and turned to remove it, allowing the bolt and return spring to be lifted out. The simple firing mechanism was attached to the bottom of the receiver, while the trigger remained in place in the wooden stock.

The Bergmann used the differential locking system, and did so by dividing the bolt and firing pin into separate units. Since the return spring thrust directly into the firing pin holder, and this, in turn, thrust into the bolt, this meant that the firing pin always stood well proud of the bolt face and was thus in position ready to strike the cartridge cap as soon as the cartridge offered resistance during the loading movement.

In order to get the design into production, an existing magazine was adopted. This was the *Trommel* or 'snail' magazine which had originally been produced for the 'long 08' Luger pistol. It was a spiral drum magazine with a long extension which slotted into the butt of the pistol in place of the conventional magazine and thus gave the pistol a 32-round reserve. This was adapted to the Bergmann gun by simply placing a sleeve around the magazine extension so that it

The Versailles Treaty forbade the postwar Reichswehr to possess submachine-guns. Some MP-18s however reached the Weimar Republic's 'Green Police', so-called for the colour of their uniforms

German stormtrooper, the cutting edge of the 1918 offensive, armed with the revolutionary Bergmann MP-18 with its characteristic snail magazine

Bergmann MP-18

Simple, strong and reliable, the MP-18 was the first true blow-back operated SMG and virtually the first to be used in combat. Development began in 1916 and 30,000 had been made by the Armistice but very few reached the German front line *Weight:* 9 lb 4 oz *Rate of fire:* 400 rpm *Muzzle velocity:* 1250 fps

The deadlocked Western Front was violently broken open in March 1918 when German stormtroopers using infiltration tactics and backed up by massive firepower prised open the Allied front-line. The Bergmann submachine-gun was an ideal weapon for fast-moving infantry.

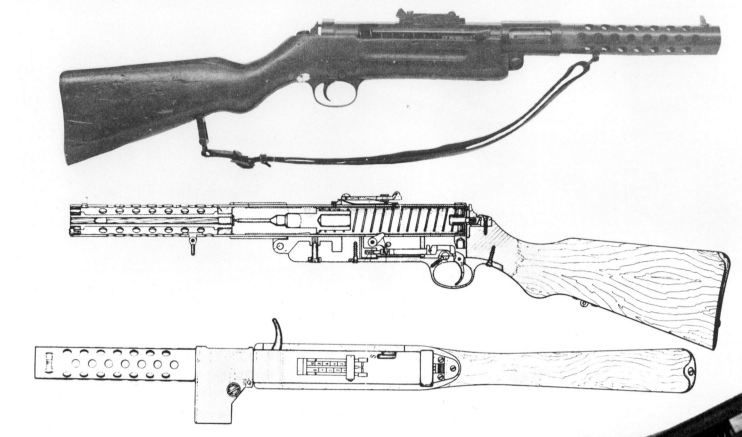

Bergmann MP-28
A direct descendant of the MP-18 but with a selector mechanism allowing single-shots. Widely exported in 7.63-mm, 9-mm, 9-mm Parabellum, 7.65-mm Parabellum and .45-in calibres, it was made under license in Spain and saw extensive service in the Civil War. (9-mm) *Weight:* 8 lb 12 oz *Rate of fire:* 500 rpm *Muzzle velocity:* 1250 fps

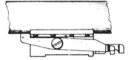

was correctly positioned for feeding. Because the butt of the Luger pistol was at an angle, the magazine housing of the Bergmann had also to be at an angle. The result of all this was less than perfect, and the only defect the gun had was in the matter of ammunition feed, due to this magazine.

Something in the order of 35,000 Bergmann MP-18s were manufactured, but reports of its use in action are uncommon, probably because of the confused nature of events in the latter months of the war and immediately afterwards. The official German Army doctrine called for the issue of these guns to all officers, all NCOs and 10% of the troops in infantry companies. Each company was to be accompanied by a submachine-gun squad with six guns, six gunners, and six men acting as ammunition carriers. These six carriers were provided with three handcarts on which to transport the ammunition, partly boxed and partly ready-loaded into spare magazines. It is

Beretta Modello 1918 9-mm
Beretta's first *Moschetto Automatico* was another modified version of the original Vilar Perosa, using the action, feed and barrel of the VP with a wooden stock and new trigger mechanism. The result was one of the world's first true submachine-guns and some were still in use during the Second World War *Weight:* 7 lb 3 oz *Rate of fire:* 900 rpm *Muzzle velocity:* 1250 fps

Moschetto Automatico OVP 9-mm
The OVP (Officine Vilar Perosa) derived from the original Modello 1915 was produced in small numbers in the '20s – using the same magazine and feed mechanism *Weight:* 8 lb 1 oz *Rate of fire:* 900 rpm *Muzzle velocity:* 1250 fps

obvious that a high ammunition consumption was anticipated, probably due to the 400 rounds-a-minute rate of fire which was theoretically possible. Moreover, there is a certain amount of similarity between this organisation and that for grenade-throwers, in which the throwers were accompanied by rifle-armed infantrymen and backed up by grenade carriers. Not only were the carriers there to speed the ammunition supply, they were also trained to step forward and take the place of the grenade throwers or submachine-gunners when these men became casualties.

It is probable that some Bergmann guns appeared on the Italian front; in any event, something moved the Italians to take another look at the Vilar Perosa and see whether it might be turned into something a trifle more practical. They gave the task to the Beretta company, who in turn handed the problem to a young designer called Tullio Marengoni. This was his introduc-

tion to submachine-guns, and he later went on to become Beretta's Chief Designer and one of history's foremost firearms designers.

What he did in this case was relatively simple. He took the Vilar Perosa as it stood, split it in half, and mounted each half into a wooden rifle stock to make two submachine-guns. The first model, the Beretta M1918, used the trigger guard with finger rest which was more or less traditional on Italian service rifles, and it also sported a folding bayonet attached to the muzzle. Fully stocked, it looked more like a carbine or short rifle than a machine-gun. Feed was from the same top-mounted magazine, while ejection was through a chute in the bottom of the stock, designed to protrude slightly so that the firer would not inadvertently grasp the stock at this point and receive a handful of hot cases when he fired. This chute looks like a conventional magazine housing, which, when no magazine is fitted, leads many people to think that the maga-

zine goes in from below.

Two other models were made: one was identical in appearance but could only fire single shots, and was for issue to police and customs guards. A third model was fitted with two triggers, one to give single shots and the other for automatic fire.

Shortly after the M1918 was put into production, the Officine Vilar Perosa decided that they would produce something similar, and did more or less the same as had Marengoni, splitting the gun in half and mounting one half into a wooden stock. A double trigger unit was fitted, the front trigger for single shots and the rear trigger for automatic fire (the Beretta trigger was copied from this). An unusual cocking system was used in which a knurled sleeve around the receiver was pulled back and pushed forward again to cock the bolt. This model, known as the 'OVP' was not produced in large numbers and did not appear in time to be used during the war.

The Thompson Submachine Gun
The Most Effective Portable Fire Arm In Existence

THE ideal weapon for the protection of large estates, ranches, plantations, etc. A combination machine gun and semi-automatic shoulder rifle in the form of a pistol. A compact, tremendously powerful, yet simply operated machine gun weighing only *seven* pounds and having only *thirty* parts. Full automatic, fired from the hip, 1,500 shots per minute. Semi-automatic, fitted with a stock and fired from the shoulder, 50 shots per minute. Magazines hold 50 and 100 cartridges.

THE Thompson Submachine Gun incorporates the simplicity and infallibility of a hand loaded weapon with the effectiveness of a machine gun. It is simple, safe, sturdy, and sure in action. In addition to its increasingly wide use for protection purposes by banks, industrial plants, railroads, mines, ranches, plantations, etc., it has been adopted by leading Police and Constabulary Forces, throughout the world and is unsurpassed for military purposes.

Information and prices promptly supplied on request

AUTO-ORDNANCE CORPORATION
302 Broadway   *Cable address: Autordco*   **New York City**

'THE RATTLE OF A THOMPSON GUN'

Once the war was over, the reaction to the submachine-gun was varied. Most armies were of the opinion that the conditions which had obtained on the Western Front in 1918 were unique, and unlikely to be repeated, and thus a weapon which had been born there due to the special conditions was unlikely to be of use in future combats. The Allied Disarmament Commission removed the submachine-gun from the German Army and prohibited its military use, although they did allow its service with Police forces. Experimental weapons were broken up and the drawings burned. One or two tentative experiments which the Allies had been making along these lines were forthwith closed down, and that was the end of the military submachine-gun, so far as the major powers were concerned, for several years.

Some people however took the trouble to look more closely at them, and one or two who had begun work during the war felt that they had to continue, if only to try and recoup some of the money they had laid out. Among them were John T Thompson amd the Auto-Ordnance Corporation.

Precisely who was responsible for the submachine-gun which commemorates the name of Brigadier-General John Tagliaferro Thompson is hard to say. Thompson had spent most of his military life in firearms design, and in 1914 he had retired to become a consulting engineer to the Remington

Chicago Historical Society

With the war over, the Auto-Ordnance Corporation tried hard to market its new weapon. The somewhat fanciful advertisement of 1922 (left) tells its own story but many more weapons find themselves in the hands of bootleggers and bank robbers than the law-abiding. The fearsome firepower of the Birger mob (above right) with their 100-round drum Thompsons and repeater shot-guns can be imagined

Thompson Prototype
Built in early 1918, the first Thompson bore little resemblance to its successors. It had two pistol grips and was tape-fed with a very high rate of fire (over 1000 rpm)

Thompson 'Annihilator' (1919 Model 1)
The first true Thompson appeared in 1919 with a box magazine and twin pistol grips. There was still no stock however

Thompson 1919 Model 2
Nearly all the famous Thompson features were incorporated in the second 1919 prototype

79

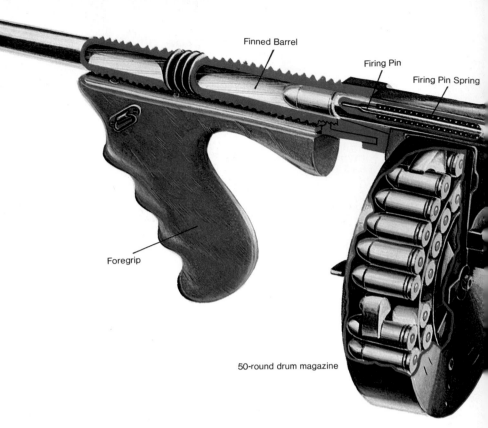

Cutts Compensator — Front Sight — Finned Barrel — Firing Pin — Firing Pin Spring

Foregrip

50-round drum magazine

Thompson M1928 .45-in

Perhaps the most famous SMG of them all – immortalised in rebel ballads and countless gangster films – the Thompson's beginnings were anything but auspicious. Conceived as a 'trench-broom' to sweep the deadlocked Western Front, the Auto-Ordnance Corporation's first product arrived too late for the war and instead became the weapon of the boot-legger and the strike-breaker. The first official military recognition came from the US Marine Corps in 1927 and the accepted model was officially named the M1928. While the Thompson was still rattling in gin-mill shoot outs, the Marines were using them in China and Central America and some found their way to wars in Spain and South America.

In 1939 the Thompson was the only SMG in mass-production outside Europe and on the outbreak of war Britain and France placed massive orders. The BEF took Thompsons to France with both drum and box magazines but the box magazine had the most military utility, night patrols reporting that the noise from a half-full drum magazine gave their position away.

The US Army also placed large orders and by the end of 1940 the Auto-Ordnance Corporation and its licensees had orders for over 318,000 weapons, but the Thompson's complexity and high quality of manufacture brought a price penalty, almost £50 per unit. Nevertheless the Thompson's reliability and efficiency in close and street-fighting made it a prized weapon and a favourite of British Commandos and US Rangers throughout the war. Similarly the fearsome reputation and aesthetic appeal of the Thompson M1928 has made it a prized weapon for guerillas and irregular forces from Ulster to Vietnam
Weight: 10 lb 12 oz *Rate of fire:* 725 rpm *Muzzle velocity:* 920 fps

Above left: Oscar Payne's original December 1920 patent for the Thompson drum magazine. A spring powered rotor pushed the bullets around a spiral track Right: John Blish's 1915 patent for his 'Breech Closure for Firearms' – the Blish lock which was at the heart of the original Thompson. Nevertheless the simplified wartime M1 discarded the device with no loss of efficiency

Left: An officer of the British Expeditionary Corps guards his Bedford platoon truck with a box magazine Thompson M1928

Imperial War Museum

Actuator

Bronze H-piece

Receiver

Recoil Spring

Lyman backsight

Safety

Sear

Trigger

Rear Grip Screw

Stock

Oil can

1 Thompson Carrying Pouch
Various methods other than violin cases
for carrying Thompsons and spare
magazines were offered including this
pouch for gun, stock and 4 × 20-round
box magazines which could be slung
from a saddle

2 Thompson Drum Magazine
Two sizes of drum were available in 50
and 100 rounds, although the bigger
drum weighed 10 lb fully loaded and
was highly impractical

Thompson Model 1921
The accessories offered for the Model
1921 included a bayonet, scabbard and
silencer

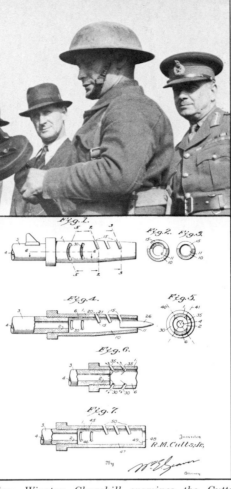

Top: Winston Churchill examines the Cutts Compensator on a British Homeguardsman's Thompson. Above: The original patent for the device which diverts the blast of the weapon upwards to compensate for its inherent tendency to 'climb' when fired in sustained bursts

company. The design of a successful military automatic rifle remained his unfulfilled ambition. His principal problem was finding a suitable breech-locking system which was not already patented and owned by one of the major arms companies. In 1915 a Commander John Blish, retired from the US Navy, patented a system of breech-locking which relied on the friction of inclined faces on a metal wedge to lock bolt and receiver together long enough to allow the breech pressure to drop. When the pressure dropped, the wedge was able to slip and thus unlock the breech. Thompson saw the Blish system as a possible answer to his rifle design, and with Blish and a financial backer, Thomas F Ryan, formed the Auto-Ordnance Corporation in 1916. A Mr Eickhoff was engaged as engineer, and in 1917, when the US entered the war and Thompson was recalled for military duty, Eickhoff continued to work on the rifle, assisted by one Oscar W Payne.

Eickhoff and Payne eventually proved that the Blish lock was impractical with any military rifle cartridge, though they were able to make it work in a gun designed to fire the standard US service .45 automatic pistol cartridge. A design was drawn up and patents were taken out in the name of 'O W Payne and the Auto-Ordnance Corporation'. The gun was perfected, but the end of the war came before it could be put up for trial.

Thompson had, by this time, abandoned his idea of a rifle and was enthusiastically pushing the new idea of a hand-held machine-gun, or, as he called it, a 'Trench Broom'. He then had a better idea (once the war was over and there were no trenches left to be swept) and coined a completely new expression; he called his invention the 'Thompson Sub-Machine Gun', and in so doing introduced the words to the world.

After a variety of tests and demonstrations, the Thompson Submachine-Gun Model 1921 went on the market, and Thompson toured the world trying to sell it. In fact Auto-Ordnance had no manufacturing facilities and they contracted with the Colt company to produce the component parts for 15,000 guns for $45 per gun. In a similar manner they got the Lyman Sight Corporation to make 15,000 sights, and Remington to produce 15,000 walnut stocks and grips. All these parts were supplied to Auto-Ordnance, who then assembled them.

Sales were relatively small, though some unfortunate publicity came about when it was found that a 'front' man in New York had bought 495 guns for the Irish Republican Army. More adverse publicity came along when the Capone Mob and other anti-social elements of the age began using Thompson guns in settling their differences.

In 1926, after a particularly audacious robbery of a US Mail truck in New Jersey, the US Post Office obtained the services of the US Marines to guard their mail shipments. The Post Office bought 250 Thompson guns and issued them to the Marines for this task. A few weeks later, when the Marines were sent to Nicaragua to help the newly-elected President Diaz, they took Thompsons with them. In 1927 more Thompsons accompanied the Marines to Shanghai.

Reports on the weapon's use in these two incidents spurred the US Navy to formalise the adoption of the gun, as the M1928. They demanded however that the rate of fire be reduced from the 1000 rounds a minute of the M1921, and Oscar Payne redesigned the bolt so as to reduce the rate to 800 rpm. The familiar front pistol grip was changed for a horizontal fore-end, and a device called the 'Cutts Compensator' on the muzzle blew a proportion of the muzzle blast upwards to force the muzzle down against the natural climb of the gun when fired automatically. Although called M1928 they were, apart from these small changes, still the Colt-made 1921s, with the date altered. There was to be no more construction of Thompsons after

the first 15,000 until the Second World War. Although various models were advertised from time to time, in the hope of boosting sales, they all came from the same source and the changes were largely cosmetic.

Several Thompsons made an appearance in the Baltic area in the 1920s, during various bouts of unrest, and this may well have had a bearing on the next design to appear, since this came from Finland. Aimo Lahti, a well-respected Finnish gun designer, produced his first submachine-gun in 1922, a model known as the *Suomi* – which simply means Finland in Finnish. This 1922 model was only made in very small numbers, and it was never placed on the market. In 1926 Lahti produced a somewhat better model which was adopted by the Finnish Army.

There were some unusual features about the Suomi. In the first place it fired the 7.65-mm Parabellum cartridge, largely because this was a service pistol cartridge of the Finnish Army. Secondly it had a quick-change barrel, and a recoil buffer which stopped the rearward movement of the bolt by compressing air inside a chamber and which, by altering the air escape port, could be adjusted to change the rate of fire. It also had a cocking handle which ran beneath the bolt and came out at the rear of the gun, so that it could be pulled back to cock the bolt and then released to run back and lie inside the gun, remaining stationary while the gun was fired.

In 1931 Lahti produced a new model which made some improvements over the 1926

Above: Austrian policemen flush out putschists on the streets of Vienna in 1934, armed with Steyr-Solothurn S1-110s

Left: Finnish troops retreating through a Karelian village towards the end of the 'Continuation War' in 1944, armed with Finnish Suomis and German Panzerfausts

Suomi M1931 9-mm
The second design by Aimo Lahti was highly influential, being exceptionally well made and widely manufactured under license. It was used in large numbers in Spain and during the Winter War
Weight: 10 lb 12 oz *Rate of fire:* 900 rpm
Muzzle velocity: 1300 fps

17. Februar 1944
Nummer 7 / 19. Jahrgang

Kölnische Illustrierte Zeitung

Preis **20** Pfg.

Druck und Verlag von M.
DuMont Schauberg, Köln
Auslandspreise auf der Rückseite

Polizeikampftruppe G

Ein Stoßtrupp geht im Lauf-
graben gegen eingebrochene
Bolschewisten vor. (Weitere
Bilder im Innern des Heftes.)

PK-Aufn.: SS-Kriegsber. Wessill (Wb)

German field police operating against Tito in the mountains of Yugoslavia armed with Erma EMPs, along with the Bergmann MP-28 a standard police and SS weapon

design. Like the 1926 it had the barrel inside a perforated cooling jacket, but instead of the peculiar curved magazine of the 1926, the new weapon adopted a straight box magazine or a drum magazine containing 71 rounds. It was chambered for the 9-mm Parabellum cartridge and was an extremely well-made and reliable weapon which, for many years, was the standard by which other designs were judged. Somewhat heavier than most submachine-guns, it compensated for this by being rather more accurate.

In Germany the memory of the Bergmann gun was kept alive by the police forces, and as early as 1920 a new design was put on paper by Louis Stange of the Rheinische Metallwaren und Maschinenfabrik of Dusseldorf, later to become better-known as Rheinmetall. Due to the restrictions imposed by the Versailles Treaty, gunmaking in Germany appeared to have very little future, and Rheinmetall arranged various connections with foreign companies during the 1920s, acquiring a considerable holding in the Oesterreichische Waffenfabrik Gesellschaft of Steyr, Austria, and setting up a subsidiary company in Switzerland called the Waffenfabrik Solothurn AG. In effect, Rheinmetall in Germany were the designers, Solothurn in Switzerland the development engineers and Steyr in Austria the production factory. Sales were attended to by yet another Swiss company, Steyr-Solothurn AG of Zurich.

Louis Stange's submachine-gun followed this route and appeared on the market bearing the Steyr-Solothurn name. It was first sold in 1930 and was extremely well-made and finished, available in almost any calibre the prospective purchaser cared to specify. It was widely sold in South America and China, and then adopted by the Austrian Army as their MP-34. This version was chambered for the powerful 9-mm 'Mauser Export' cartridge, but when Austria was absorbed into the Third Reich most of the MP-34s were rebarrelled to 9-mm Parabellum calibre. The gun was also purchased by the Portuguese Army in 1935, chambered for 7.65-mm Parabellum, their standard pistol round at the time, and the Portuguese bought the last batch ever sold, in 1942, these being chambered for 9 mm Parabellum. Although no longer used by the army, the Portuguese Guarda Nacional de Republica and Guarda Fiscal are still using them.

Operation of the Steyr-Solothurn was by the usual blow-back system, with the return spring lying in a tube which ran through the length of the butt-stock. An interesting detail was the provision of a magazine loader built into the magazine housing. This weapon was generally supplied in calibres such as 7.63-mm Mauser and 9-mm Steyr, in which the ammunition came pre-packed in ten-round chargers for loading into the appropriate pistols. In order to get the rounds into the submachine-gun magazine, it would have been necessary to strip them one by one from the chargers and load them into the magazine. In order to speed up the process the magazine housing has a charger guide and cartridge slot on top and, underneath, a housing into which the empty magazine fits. All that is necessary is to fit the empty magazine below, place the clip of cartridges in the top, and then sweep the cartridge out of the charger and into the magazine with the thumb.

Since the German police were allowed the use of submachine-guns, Hugo Schmeisser made some improvements to his MP-18 design in order to do away with some of the wartime improvisations. His first change was the magazine and its housing. The housing was changed to a right-angled unit at the left of the gun, and a straight box magazine replaced the peculiar 'snail' magazine of the original design. Then in 1928 he improved it again, calling it the MP-28, and incorporating a single-shot facility and an adjustable backsight.

The mid-1920s produced another submachine-gun designer destined for fame, Heinrich Vollmer who, together with Berthold Giepel, patented a new weapon in 1927. The novelty in his design lay in the construction of the bolt and return spring as a self-contained unit. The bolt carried a telescoping tubular spring casing on its rear end, inside which was the return spring, and concealed within the bolt, the firing pin and its housing. Thus when the weapon was dismantled there was no danger of the spring shooting from the receiver, the entire bolt and spring unit being lifted out as one piece. Giepel was the manager of the Erfurt Maschinenwerk, or 'Ermawerke' of Erfurt, and in 1930 this company began making the Vollmer design, marketing it as the 'Erma' submachine-gun. It was available in a variety of calibres and was unusual in having a telescoping monopod built in to the forward pistol grip. This could be extended to rest on the ground and support the gun when being fired from the prone position. The barrel was not concealed by any form of jacket, while the box magazine was entered into the left side of the receiver.

After seeing this product on to the market, Vollmer made some changes, the principal one being the addition of a perforated barrel jacket and a bolt-locking safety catch mounted on the front right of the receiver. By switching this to the 'Safe' position, a lug entered a specially-cut slot in the bolt and firmly anchored it, preventing any movement. This was a useful addition, since by this time one of the defects of the simple blow-back system had become apparent. If a blow-back operated gun were dropped butt down, the inertia of the heavy bolt would be sufficient to make the bolt compress the return spring and so move back in the receiver. Not far enough to run over the sear and thus be held, but far enough to go beyond the magazine, so that when the spring forced the bolt back it took a cartridge with it, loaded it and fired it, to the astonishment of whoever happened to have dropped the weapon in the first place. Although Vollmer saw the need for a safety device as early as 1935 – when the first of his new 'EMP' (Erma Maschinen Pistole) appeared – it seems to have escaped many other designers for several years.

The last important design of the early 1930s was a Swiss development. Schweizerische Industrie Gesellschaft (SIG) of Neuhausen were a well-established arms firm with experience of automatic weapons design and, during the early 1920s, they had taken out a licence from Hugo Schmeisser to manufacture his MP-18. Indeed, it seems probable that they were responsible for changing the magazine from the sloped-in snail to the square-mounted box and that Schmeisser followed their example when he redesigned the MP-18 for the German police. After this, however, they decided to go back to first principles and design their own weapon, and three men, named Gaetzi, End and Kiraly set to work. The result was the Model MKMO which appeared in 1933, and which incorporated some unusual ideas.

The MKMO was fully-stocked in wood and resembled a short rifle at first glance. The most obvious novelty was that the box magazine, beneath the gun, could be folded forward, together with its housing, into a slot in the stock for carrying, being quickly swung back into the firing position when required. It was available in various calibres, one being the 9 mm 'Mauser Export'. This is the most powerful 9-mm pistol cartridge ever made in quantity and as a result the SIG engineers decided that something better than the usual differential locking was needed but it was a difficult and expensive weapon to manufacture, and as a result it was not a commercial success.

The first units into occupied Warsaw in 1939 included these German police armed with MP-28s

Erma EMP 9-mm
The German Army was equipped with the Ermawerke's first SMG in 1936 and a small number of these weapons went to Spain. Production ended in 1938 and some were used by SS 'foreign legions' during the Second World War *Weight:* 9 lb 2 oz *Rate of fire:* 500 rpm *Muzzle-velocity:* 1250 fps

THE SHOOTING STARTS

The Gran Chaco war, fought sporadically among the South American deserts and jungles from 1932 to 1935, was the first time that submachine-guns were brought into conflict with each other, and they were found to be ideal weapons for jungle fighting. However, this war raised little interest outside South America, and it was not until the Spanish Civil War that the potential of the submachine-gun was recognised in Europe. Not only did both sides in this bitter conflict buy whatever weapons they could lay their hands on, but local manufacturers turned out designs, and Germany, Russia and Italy, intent upon having their latest ideas tested in the field, were not slow in providing supplies of various designs.

Most of the volunteer forces involved appear to have been more enthusiastic than knowledgeable, and in these peculiar circumstances the submachine-gun showed itself to some advantage. It was easy to take untrained men and teach them to use a submachine-gun. It rarely went wrong and when it did it was either easily mended or cheap enough to throw away, and it was fairly catholic in the ammunition it fired. These aspects were particularly noted by the Germans and the Soviets, both of whom were examining the probability of having to arm vast numbers of men quickly in the future, and both these nations set to work to develop a standard submachine-gun for military adoption. The Italians gave the matter rather less attention, as did the French, while the British and Americans appear to have ignored the lesson completely.

The Suomi, Erma and Bergmann weapons appeared in Spain in some numbers, and since there was a well-established gunmaking industry in Spain it was not long before some native models appeared. One of the first was the 'Gollat', which in 1935–36 was made in small numbers in Eibar, the gun-making centre of Spain. This resembled a slightly lengthened Bergmann and appears to have been more or less copied from that design.

More original was the design which came from the factory of Bonifacio Echeverria of Eibar, a prominent company which was famous for its 'Star' automatic pistols. The Star S135 submachine-gun was designed by Suinaga and Irusta, two executives of the company, and it was unusual in many respects. There were two control levers on the side which could be set to give single-shot fire, a slow rate of automatic fire, a fast rate of automatic fire, or a safe position. Instead of the usual blow-back action, the breech was securely closed and locked before the firing pin moved, and safety was controlled by a delaying action in the bolt mechanism. A vertically-moving lock plate was cammed up to engage in recesses in the receiver by the action of a loose and heavy hammer unit as the bolt came to a stop on closing the breech. On firing, the rearward movement of the bolt had to cam this plate down again, against the inertia of the hammer unit and the pressure of the return spring. All this, plus the complication of a spring escapement unit to reduce the rate of fire meant that there were about eighty different pieces to the weapon, which in turn meant that it was difficult to manufacture and equally difficult to repair when it went wrong, factors which go a long way in accounting for its lack of enthusiastic reception in military circles.

Another local product was the Labora, probably the best of the Spanish weapons of the time. It was made by the Industrias de Guerra de Cataluna, a factory set up to produce weapons during the war and which closed down shortly afterwards. It was an extremely high quality weapon, particularly in view of the circumstances of its origin and manufacture, and this can only be accounted for by the system of gunmaking which obtained in Spain at that time, a system in which most of the work was done by hand in small outside workshops, only the principal machining and assembly being done in the factory. There was an ample supply of skilled labour, a force which, even under the stresses of war, were so imbued with their craft that they turned out a highly-finished product.

The Labora was solidly built, with a heavy machined receiver and a barrel having broad and rounded cooling ribs. The magazine housing was unusually large and doubled as a forward hand grip. The mechanism was simple blow-back, with a selector to allow single shots or automatic fire. The bolt assembly was very light and the return spring was very stiff, a combination which accounts for its high rate of fire, about 750 rpm.

Armoured Tactics

In Germany the Army had bought handfuls of submachine-guns from various sources in order to test them, but, like almost every other army of the day, they were unable to fit this new weapon into the existing tactical framework. However, by the early 1930s the tactics of the armoured division were slowly being worked out by Guderian and others. While most countries considered the tank to be an object apart, the German Army began to study the tank in cooperation with other arms of the service in a balanced and mutually-supporting independent force, the force which was to become the Panzer Divisions.

The MP-40 has become the almost universal symbol of the German soldier of the Second World War – whether equipping the infantry who invaded Russia (left) or the paratroops that fell on Crete (right)

Labora 9-mm
Manufactured in the last few months of the Civil War, the Spanish Labora was built to very high standards by traditional gun-smithing methods
Weight: 9 lb 6 oz *Rate of fire:* 750 rpm *Muzzle velocity:* 1300 fps

The motorized infantry of this force was going to have to be a fast-moving hard-hitting spearhead, very much the same sort of force which von Hutier had predicated with his Storm Troops of 1918, and, from this appreciation, it followed that the armament of the force would have to be along similar lines, with plenty of automatic fire-power. What was needed, it was eventually decided, was a good submachine-gun. At about the same time the 'observers' in Spain were reporting back on the utility of the submachine-gun in arming conscript armies. One thing led to another and in 1938 the German High Command sent for Berthold Giepel of Ermawerke and told him to make them a submachine-gun as soon as possible.

Herr Giepel had seen this coming, and he and Vollmer already had a prototype ready. A few finishing touches, military tests, and the weapon was approved for production in the summer of 1938, becoming the Maschinen Pistole 1938 or MP-38. Next to the Thompson, the MP-38 (and its successor the MP-40) is probably the most recognisable submachine-gun ever made. It virtually became the trademark of the German soldier.

Hugo Schmeisser

It might also be pointed out that these two were the most remarkably misnamed weapons in the history of firearms. Throughout the war, up to the present day, and doubtless for years to come, they have been called the 'Schmeisser'. Yet Hugo Schmeisser had nothing whatever to do with the design. It is doubly unfortunate that the one well-known gun that Schmeisser *did* design is always called the Bergmann. The MP-38 was based totally on the Vollmer telescoping bolt assembly and other features designed by him and Giepel. The only contact Schmeisser ever made with the weapon was to oversee manufacture when the quantity became too great for Ermawerke and the task was contracted out to the Haenel company who employed Schmeisser.

The MP-38 broke new ground in several directions. It was the first submachine-gun to be taken into major use by a top-class army; it was the first weapon to abandon the use of wood for its 'furniture', being made entirely of metal and plastic; and it was the first to use a folding steel stock. In spite of its modern appearance it was still made by traditional gunsmithing methods, its corrugated appearance arising from grooves machined in the steel receiver in order to lighten it. Manufacture was a slow business involving much machining and milling and precision work, and it was therefore redesigned with a view to speeding up production. The receiver was formed from a sheet-metal stamping, and interior components were similarly stamped out, assembly being by welding and pressing. This became the MP-40 and the principal distinguishing feature between them is the smooth receiver of the MP-40 instead of corrugated as in the MP-38.

The submachine-gun was an ideal weapon for guerrilla warfare and these Italian partisans display a rich collection including (from left to right) an MP-44 assault rifle, Sten and MP-40. (opposite page) Top: Another captured weapon, an MP-40 in the delicate hands of a Maquisard. Bottom: Loading box from drum magazines for an MP-38

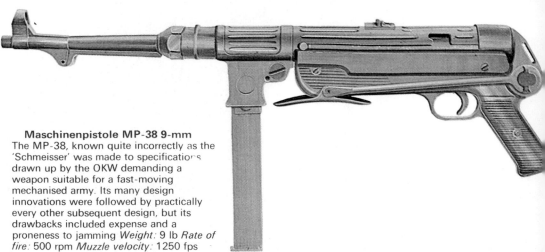

Maschinenpistole MP-38 9-mm
The MP-38, known quite incorrectly as the 'Schmeisser' was made to specifications drawn up by the OKW demanding a weapon suitable for a fast-moving mechanised army. Its many design innovations were followed by practically every other subsequent design, but its drawbacks included expense and a proneness to jamming *Weight:* 9 lb *Rate of fire:* 500 rpm *Muzzle velocity:* 1250 fps

Maschinenpistole MP-40 9-mm

Like its counterparts, the Sten and the M3, the original MP-38 design still left room for improvement and re-working for simpler mass-production. The MP-40 was substantially the same as its predecessor but its construction utilised a minimum of machining operations and a maximum of sub-assemblies sub-contracted to a myriad of minor firms throughout the Reich. The use of high-grade steel was kept to a minimum and many parts were made of spot-welded stampings *Weight:* 8 lb 12 oz *Rate of fire:* 500 rpm *Muzzle velocity:* 1250 fps

The Soviet Army had been looking at submachine-guns since the middle 1920s, but the first model to be adopted in any numbers was the PPD-34, a design by Degtyarev, which entered service in 1934. Generally speaking it was based on the tried and tested Bergmann MP-18 design, and most production models were sent to Spain in 1936–37. Early models of this gun used a 25-round box magazine, but this was soon supplemented by an unusual 71-round drum type with a long extension in order to fit it into the housing designed for a box magazine.

Experience in Spain showed that there were some improvements which could usefully be made to the PPD-34, and Degtyarev redesigned the gun completely, producing the PPD-40. The first thing to go was the odd extension on the drum magazine, and a fresh design, more or less a copy of that used with the Finnish Suomi, was adopted, a drum which slotted straight in to a space left in the receiver and fore-end. The mechanism was changed from the simple inertia-locked blow-back of the Bergmann pattern to one in which the breech was closed and the bolt had stopped moving before the cartridge was fired. The firing pin was actuated by a cam lever in the bolt so that as the bolt closed, so the cam was rotated to give a blow to the firing pin. It was, in effect, an automatic safety device which prevented the cartridge from being fired unless the bolt was properly closed.

Although a simple design, the PPD-40 was still machined from bar steel, but when the pressures of war increased it was dropped in favour of weapons capable of being made more quickly and cheaply. Like all Soviet submachine-guns, it was chambered for the 7.62-mm Soviet automatic pistol cartridge, which is almost identical with the 7.63-mm Mauser round. One advantage of this was that the calibre was the same as that of the standard military rifles, and thus existing barrel-making machinery could be utilised.

Novosti

Russian cavalry operating behind the German lines confer with their maps, their PPD-40s close to hand

PPD-40

The original PPD was re-designed in 1940 for simpler mass production and was first used in Finland. A new 71-round box pagazine was introduced and the barrel jacket cooling slots were simplified. Production only lasted until late 1941 after which it was replaced by the PPSh model *Weight:* 8 lb 2 oz *Rate of fire:* 800 rpm *Muzzle velocity:* 1600 fps

PPD-34/38

Tho first model of the Pistolet Pulyemet Degtyarev (machine-pistol designed by V A Degtyarev) appeared in 1934 incorporating several features of contemporary Finnish and German weapons. The second model featured a simpler barrel jacket *Weight:* 8 lb 4 oz *Rate of fire:* 800 rpm *Muzzle velocity:* 1600 fps

Russian paratroops display their new medals following an investiture – and show off a selection of submachine-guns including PPD-40s and PPSh-41s

Beretta M1938A 9-mm
Looking similar to the Model 10 1918, but in fact
an entirely new design. It was well-made and
reliable and continued in mass-production until
1950 *Weight:* 9 lb 4 oz *Rate of fire:* 600 rpm
Muzzle velocity: 1250 fps

*Above and right: Beretta M1938As in the hands
of Italian mountain troops. This gun was widely
used throughout the war – with the Italians in
North Africa and Russia and by the Germans
and other satellites*

The Italian Army now expressed a desire for a submachine-gun, as with Germany and Russia, a designer was ready with the answer. Marengoni, Beretta's designer, had been sporadically working away at sub-machine-guns designs since 1918, and he now produced his Model 1938A, one of the best designs ever seen. It went into production in early 1938 and, in one form or another, stayed in production until 1950.

The M1938A used a short wooden stock and had the barrel concealed inside a perforated jacket, at the front end of which was a simple muzzel compensator. Early models were provided with attachments for a bayonet, but this was more ornamental than useful on a submachine-gun and its use was later abandoned. A box magazine fitted in from below, and firing was by the same two trigger arrangement seen on the Model 1918, the forward trigger giving single shots and the rear trigger automatic fire. Unusually, it was another weapon in which the bolt was closed and stationary before the cartridge was fired, a spring-loaded firing pin inside the bolt being released automatically as the bolt closed.

The M1938A appeared in three distinct versions. The first, described above, was recognisable by the long slots in the jacket. The second had round perforations in the jacket and what appears to be three triggers. In fact, the rear 'trigger' is a safety lock which prevents the automatic fire trigger from being used accidentally. The third, and most common model, had the second pattern of barrel jacket, two triggers, and a new muzzle compensator with four ports instead of two; it also dispensed with the bayonet.

The only other major force to adopt a submachine-gun before the outbreak of war in 1939 was the French Army. They adopted the MAS-38 in 1938, a design from the Manufacture d'Armes de St Etienne, from whence came the initials MAS. In the event, production did not begin until 1939 and the first supplies actually went to the *Gardes Mobiles* and not to the army. It was an odd-looking weapon, due to its construction. The bolt recoiled down a tunnel in the wooden butt and, in order to make the gun convenient to hold and aim, the barrel had to be set at an angle to the butt, which meant that the face of the bolt had to be cut at an angle.

Odd Cartridge

Another unusual feature was the method of applying the safety catch – to lock the bolt safe in either the forward or rear position, the trigger is pushed forward.

Nevertheless, the MAS-38 was a good and reliable weapon with a reputation for accuracy. Its only fault lay in the odd cartridge it fired, the French Service 7.65-mm *Longue*. A weak round and a small one, it was adopted simply because at that time it was the standard French pistol cartridge. It has been said, and there seems some justification for it, that if the gun had been chambered for a more sensible cartridge, such as the 9-mm Parabellum, it might have gained wider recognition and a greater reputation.

Contrary to common belief, the British Army had not entirely closed its eyes to the submachine-gun and it had, during the 1930s, tested just about every model in existence. But as with the Germans, the stumbling block was in the question of its tactical use – how to fit this individualistic weapon into a framework of training and drill which had already been evolved. Another drawback was that over the years the testing authorities had become conditioned to looking for long-lasting attributes in weapons and a quality of manufacture which would ensure that it passed any conceivable test and would virtually never break down. This was not the quality of weapon that was being produced, and consequently the British Army was always being told that as soon as a good enough weapon appeared, they would be issued with it, but they would have to wait.

During a murder hunt across the roofs of postwar Paris a flic looks businesslike with his MAS-38

PM9

The extraordinary French PM9 was built after the war and had a unique action with the bolt acting as a connecting rod turning a fly wheel – allowing a short overall body length and a variable rate of fire. The complication however produced little advantage at high cost *Weight:* 5 lb 8 oz *Rate of fire:* 750 rpm *Muzzle velocity:* 1200 fps

PM9 Action

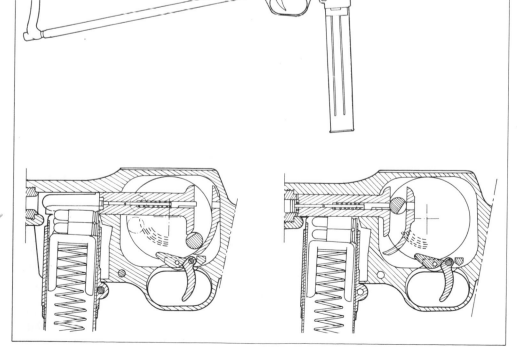

Gepisztoly 39M 9-mm
Fully stocked like a rifle and able to take a bayonet, the Hungarian 39M was unusually bulky but built to the highest standards and was a reliable and accurate weapon. The first issues were made to the Hungarian *Honvèd* in 1941 and they were extensively used on the Eastern Front *Weight:* 8 lb 3 oz *Rate of fire:* 750 rpm *Muzzle velocity:* 1475 fps

Right: The complicated trigger mechanism of the BSA built Kiraly design. The Hungarian M39 used a straightforward sear system

Gespiztoly 43M 9-mm
Folding stock paratroopers version of the 39M Hungarian submachine-gun

The submachine-gun had been a child of the First World War but was an adolescent in the '30s where it was tested and proved in numerous small wars. Right: A Chinese infantryman carries a Bergmann MP-28 during the war with Japan

In September 1939 the time for waiting ran out. In May 1939 the War Office had had its attention drawn to a submachine-gun manufactured by the Danuvia Arms company of Budapest, which the Birmingham Small Arms company had obtained a licence to make in Britain. It was designed by Kiraly and, as a result, leaned heavily on the SIG MKMO for its inspiration. The magazine housing was fixed, instead of folding, and as it carried 40 rounds of 9-mm Mauser, this meant a somewhat bulky protrusion. The two-part bolt of the SIG weapon had been highly modified; it still used two sections but the two were separated by a lever arrangement to the bolt head. When the bolt body was forward, the lever was rotated into a recess in the receiver and locked the bolt, and it did not unlock until the bolt body had recoiled some distance.

The whole gun however was a sound design and BSA were of the opinion that they could make them for no more than £5 each, which was a remarkably cheap price for such a gun. The worst feature was a complicated rate of fire reducer which involved a flywheel, springs and gears, but in spite of this the weapon performed well on trial. But for some unexplained reason there was a total lack of interest shown by the War Office, and eventually BSA gave up the licence. Kiraly took his gun back, made some modifications in the design based on the comments made in Britain, and it became the Hungarian Army's Model 1939 thereafter.

Gangster-Gun
So in September 1939 when the British Army went to war, it still had no submachine-gun, and in December 1939 the Army made an official request to the Ordnance Board for 'a supply of machine-carbine or gangster guns' to be sent to France for use by patrols. Seven guns, various specimens which had been bought for test and placed in store, were sent to France for trials, and a variety of projects were examined. The Ordnance Board pointed out that no weapon demanding a special supply of ammunition would be contemplated, which restricted the field to weapons chambered for the service .303 rifle, .38 revolver or 7.92-mm machine-gun cartridges, none of which were the slightest use in submachine-guns.

But by January 1940 this ideal had to be discarded. The Ordnance Board came to the conclusion that the best design was the Suomi, but since the Finns were by then fighting for their lives against the Soviet Army, they were unlikely to find time to supply submachine-guns to Britain. The next best was the Thompson, 'the most costly of its class, costing £50 a gun and involving dollar exchange. Also it is the most complicated and elaborate as regards manufacture. It shoots high unless fitted with a special muzzle compensator which costs $20 . . .' But it was the only weapon which could be procured, and orders were given for 450 guns and a supply of ammunition. The French Army had already ordered 3000 guns, costing $75,000 in November 1939, and this was causing some disturbance in America.

Thompson M1 .45-in
The design of the Thompson M1928 was twenty years old when it was rushed into mass production on the outbreak of war in Europe. In 1941 it was extensively redesigned for cheaper and faster production and the so called 'Blish-lock' was discarded along with the drum magazine and forward hand grip. The weapon worked just as well in its simplified form and was standardised by the US Army as the M1 in April 1942. The further modified M1A1 made the firing pin integral with the bolt and dispensed with the hammer *Weight:* 10 lb 8 oz *Rate of fire:* 700 rpm *Muzzle velocity:* 920 fps

Left: British troops armed with a Thompson M1 and an M1928A dig into the ruins of a Normandy village

Thompson Model T2
An unsuccessful attempt by the Auto-Ordnance Corporation to compete for the contract awarded to the M3

In 1930 the Auto-Ordnance Corporation had been scraping along with minimal sales, and Thomas Ryan, the backer, had decided to run the business down. He bought out Thompson and Thompson's son and set about closing the operation down. He was less than pleased with the 'gangster' image and he had seen very little return on the $1,500,000 he had put into the business. By the end of 1938 10,300 guns had been sold and 4700 of the original 15,000 batch remained awaiting buyers. Ryan still wanted out, and he sold the whole business to a man called Russell Maguire, a sharp businessman who was gambling on the possibility of a war in Europe and, with it, a possible market for the Thompson gun.

Having bought the company, Maguire ordered stocks of steel and began advertising the gun, but he ran into trouble when he approached Colt to get them to make some more. Colt, too, were displeased with the 'gangster' image, and they wanted no part of the Thompson gun. Eventually, Maguire made a deal with the Savage Arms Corporation to make 10,000 guns. No sooner had he done this than the British Army's order went up from 450, in rapid steps, to a total of 107,500, the French added another 3000 to their order and the US Army also ordered 20,450 guns.

This sudden bonanza came too late for the inventor. In June 1940 John T Thompson died of a heart attack at the age of 70, just as his 'Trench Broom' was about to fulfil his dreams.

With these massive orders, and the promise of more to come, Maguire set up his own Auto-Ordnance company factory in August 1940 and went into production, just as the US Army increased its order to 319,000 guns. At about this time the Savage Company engineers pointed out to Maguire that the celebrated 'Blish Lock' was a complete waste of time and money, and modifying the gun to do away with the lock, turning it into a straight blow-back weapon, would mean a cheaper and simpler gun, a more reliable gun, and one which could be made a good deal faster.

There was nothing new in this suggestion. Eickhoff and Payne had pointed it out to Thompson as far back as 1919, before the first 'Tommy-gun' had been made, but Thompson was horrified at the idea. The Blish lock was the 'mystery' at the heart of the Thompson, and to do away with it was unthinkable. Maguire's reaction was the same; without the Blish lock, the Thompson gun wasn't the Thompson, and he said so to Savage. But Savage were more concerned with what they saw as a waste of Uncle Sam's money for a design gimmick which wasn't necessary, and they threatened to

put their own design of submachine-gun on to the market to undercut the Thompson unless Auto-Ordnance agreed to the change. And so in early 1942 a simplified Thompson was tested and found to be completely satisfactory, and this design was standardised by the US Army as the 'Thompson Submachine-gun M1' in April 1942.

For the next two years, production continued, and as the volume increased, the price came down with a rush. In 1921 the gun had sold for $225; in 1939 the contract price to the French was $250, which soon dropped to $210. In 1942 the last of the M1928 models (with the Blish lock) were made for $70 each, and the M1 was made for $45. Even so, Maguire did so well from the business that in 1942 the US Government proceeded against him for excess profits and managed to get $6,500,000 back from him. Altogether 1,750,000 complete guns, plus spares to make another 250,000, were built during the war years.

But even at the reduced prices, the Thompson was still an expensive gun, and the British Army were anxious to find a design they could put into production in Britain. By August 1940, after the disaster of Dunkirk and with a German invasion expected hourly, some form of submachine-gun was a pressing priority, and after much discussion it was decided that the quickest solution would be to take an existing design and copy it. The design selected was the Bergmann MP-28, on the grounds that it was a simple and straightforward manufacturing proposition and, since it was an enemy weapon, there would be no problems about licences or patent infringement. The gun was slightly redesigned to suit British manufacturing methods, called the Lanchester Carbine, and orders were given for the manufacture of 50,000 commencing in December 1940. The gun was to be in 9-mm Parabellum calibre, and 110 million rounds of ammunition were ordered from the USA since no facilities existed for production of such quantities in Britain.

The scheduled production date, though, came and went and the Lanchester was still being worked on. Tests had shown problems with certain types of ammunition, and it was vital to have a submachine-gun which would not only fire the issued rounds but which could, in emergency, fire captured enemy ammunition of the correct type. While this work was going on, the Armaments Design Department of Woolwich Arsenal were working on a design of their own, and in January 1941 they announced that a simplified submachine-gun had been designed and prototypes manufactured.

A sailor of the Royal New Zealand Navy during the Korean War (note the MiG painted on his helmet), armed with a Lanchester submachine-gun

Lanchester Mk I 9-mm
A direct copy of the German MP-28 designed by Hugo Schmeisser, the Lanchester was rushed into production as a stop-gap weapon in 1941 but was only issued to the Royal Navy *Weight:* 9 lb 9 oz *Rate of fire:* 600 rpm *Muzzle velocity:* 1250 fps

The Sten : Crude but Deadly

This was the 'Machine-Carbine N.O.T. 40/1' which had been designed by Major R V Shepherd and Mr H J Turpin of the Small Arms Design Department at Enfield. The gun was demonstrated on 10 January 1941 and again on 21 January, after which orders were given for an immediate full-scale trial and a rapid decision as to whether the Lanchester should go ahead as planned or whether it should be dropped in favour of the new gun.

The report of the trial was made on 31 January, in which it was said that the weapon 'appears to be fundamentally sound and functions satisfactorily and accurately', and it was decided to adopt it as the standard submachine-gun for the Army and Royal Air Force. Production of the Lanchester would be curtailed and this gun would go to the Royal Navy.

The N.O.T. 40/1 now became the Sten Gun, the name being derived from the two designers and the Enfield factory, and in June 1941 the first supplies were produced. This, the Mk 1, had some small degrees of refinement still. A flash hider-cum-compensator on the muzzle; a wooden stock with folding front grip and a barrel jacket with protectors for the foresight. The butt was a skeleton of steel tubing, and the cocking handle could be turned down into a slot in the receiver to lock the bolt to the rear for safety. The mechanical side of the weapon was extremely simple – the receiver was simply a steel tube with a magazine housing and barrel jacket welded to it. Inside the tube was a bolt with fixed firing pin and return spring. The trigger mechanism was pinned together from steel stampings.

Once production had begun it was felt that some of the refinements could be trimmed away in order to make things even easier, and the wooden fore-end was abandoned, the trigger mechanism now being covered with a stamped steel housing. The flash hider was also abandoned, and the butt was made from half-round steel strip. This was adopted as the Mk 1*, but few were made, since the simplification process had been carried still further to produce the Mk 2, the Sten which became the most common version of them all.

While the mechanism of the Mk 2 was the same, the method of putting it all together had changed. The barrel jacket was discarded and the short barrel was retained in the receiver by a screwed-in short jacket which doubled as a hand-grip. The butt became a single steel tube with a flat plate welded on to the end, and the magazine housing could be rotated through 90° to close the feed and extraction ports and thus prevent dirt entering the weapon, also making it easier to pack. By removing the barrel and butt and turning the magazine housing, the Sten Mk 2 could be crammed

Dug into the Dutch earth on the Arnhem defence perimeter, a British paratrooper takes aim with a Sten Mk 5, the first time this model was used in battle

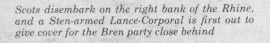

into a surprisingly small space. Over two million were made, the Royal Ordnance Factory at Fazackerly, Liverpool, turning out 20,000 a week at one stage. It was first used in combat by Canadian troops in the attack on Dieppe on 19 August 1942.

While the original Sten was strictly utility, later models, as will be shown, improved both safety and appearance and were eventually as good as anyone could want. While it was important as a weapon of war, it was equally important as a symbol. It broke what might be called the 'gunsmith barrier'. Here at last was a weapon adopted in vast numbers by a major power which was stamped out, welded up, and churned out by the million with scant regard for niceties of form or finish, a weapon which abandoned the traditional methods of manufacture and the traditional standards of longevity and engineering so long associated with firearms in general and military weapons in particular. The sten was designed to be used, and used hard, until it broke down or wore out, and then to be thrown away. It was quicker and cheaper to make a new one than to try and repair the old.

The submachine-gun was, of course, the ideal weapon for Commandos and other raiding forces, and as early as 1940 they had expressed a desire to have a silent weapon for picking off sentries so as to be able to surprise their objectives. The first such weapon to be issued was a specially silenced Thompson, but the addition of a large muffler unit to the already heavy Thompson made an awkward handful and it was never made in any quantity. But the Sten was a more attractive proposition, and a silenced version, the Mk 2S, appeared in 1942.

The problem of silencing a weapon is not simply a matter of muffling the noise of the discharge. If the bullet is travelling faster than the speed of sound it generates a sonic wave in front which is audible to as great a degree as the noise of the cartridge, and this has to be catered for. The silenced Thompson was a simple matter, since the .45 bullet was subsonic and caused no problems. But the 9-mm Parabellum bullet moved at supersonic speeds and it was necessary to reduce the muzzle velocity as well as silence the cartridge. The barrel of the Sten was pierced by a number of small holes, and then enclosed in a tubular casing containing rubber baffles. As the shot was fired, gas leaked out of the barrel holes, behind the bullet, and so reduced the velocity. Once the bullet left the muzzle, it was still inside the silencer casing, passing through the baffles, and the blast, which would normally give rise to noise, was shuffled back and forth between the baffles until its speed was reduced to a silent level before being finally allowed to escape to the atmosphere. The effect was that at 50 ft from the gun, all that could be heard was the clank of the bolt going forward. Moreover, the silencer also concealed the flash at night.

The only drawbacks were that due to the reduced velocity the gun was only accurate to about 100 yards, though this was of little matter in the circumstances of its use, and that it could only be fired in single shots, except in dire emergency. Firing it automatic caused the silencer to vibrate out of alignment with the barrel and also built up pressure too rapidly inside the baffles, all of which meant that after three or four shots, the baffles were destroyed and the gun was no longer silent.

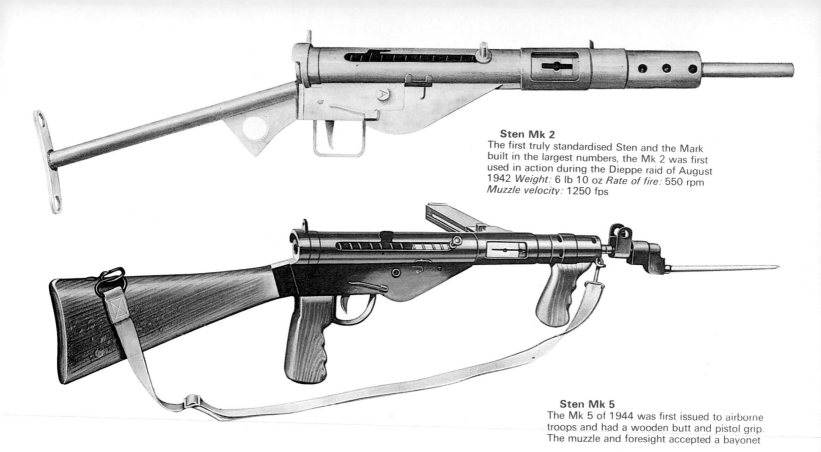

Sten Mk 2
The first truly standardised Sten and the Mark built in the largest numbers, the Mk 2 was first used in action during the Dieppe raid of August 1942 *Weight:* 6 lb 10 oz *Rate of fire:* 550 rpm *Muzzle velocity:* 1250 fps

Sten Mk 5
The Mk 5 of 1944 was first issued to airborne troops and had a wooden butt and pistol grip. The muzzle and foresight accepted a bayonet

Men of the Polish Home Army on the streets of Warsaw during the 1944 uprising armed with parachute-delivered British Stens

Sten Mk 2
The Sten was manufactured with both a single strut shoulder stock and a skeleton butt in mild steel

Austen Mk I 9-mm
The first Sten-guns to arrive in Australia were the
basis for a new home-built weapon which became
known as the Austen from Australian Sten. The
Austen with its unwieldy buttstock copied from
the German MP-38 was never as popular as the
Owen *Weight:* 8 lb 2 oz *Rate of fire:* 500 rpm
Muzzle velocity: 1250 fps

Sten Gun with silencer

The Sten was a
favourite Special
Operations Executive
weapon; cheap reliable, and
easy to conceal. Fitting it with a silencer made it
even more suitable for clandestine operations.
Its drawback was that full automatic fire soon
burnt out the silencer, restricting it to the semi-
automatic role

Right: A French Maquisard *lies in wait with a
Sten Mk 2. Stens were reliable and durable and
could be easily broken down for concealment.
From the Massif Central to the sewers of Warsaw
they were a favourite weapon of those who resisted
the New Order in Hitler's Europe*

Australia's Own Firepower for Jungle Fighting

Owen Mk I 9-mm
The principle SMG of the Australian Army entered production on the eve of the Pacific War, and in spite of some eccentric features, was highly popular with all who used it *Weight:* 9 lb 5 oz *Rate of fire:* 700 rpm *Muzzle velocity:* 1250 fps

The Sten gave rise to a number of copies and near-copies, since it represented just about the rock-bottom minimum for a service weapon. In 1940 the Australian Army began looking for submachine-guns. Britain could be of little help since they were on the same search, and the Americans could only offer the Thompson, and not many of those. Self-help was the only solution, and two local designs eventually appeared.

The Austen Gun, as the name implies, was the 'Australian Sten' though it was a rather more elegant product than the original Sten. Broadly speaking, it managed to amalgamate the best features of the Sten with those of the German MP-38. The MP-38 provided the collapsible butt, the telescoping mainspring housing and the pistol grip, while the Sten provided the basic layout, barrel and magazine. A front pistol grip was added, and the method of folding and locking the butt was actually an improvement on the original Erma design.

For all this excellence the Austen was unpopular. It is difficult to say why, but (small as it may seem) one fault was the length of the butt. It had to be long in order to fold around the front pistol grip, and this slight additional length meant that the gun was awkward to hold and to aim properly. Whatever the reason, the Austen was never as popular as the other Australian design, the Owen Gun. The weakest part of the Austen was the same as that of the Sten – the magazine. This was a single-column box, the dimensions of which proved to be critical. Any deformation of the lip resulted in a mis-feed, and any dirt inside the box inevitably led to jams.

The Mk 1 Austen went into production in the middle of 1942 and about 20,000 were made before production stopped in March 1945. By that time a Mk 2 had been developed and had also gone into production. This was considerably different in appearance, though it retained the same mechanical features as the Mk 1. The principal change lay in a unique method of assembly. The gun receiver was a thin steel tube and this was supported in a receiver frame of cast light alloy. This, light but very strong, surrounded the receiver and working parts and protected them from damage while allowing the whole gun to be manufactured very simply. Although a sound design, the Mk 2 never got into volume production, since the war ended shortly after it had been introduced.

The other, and in fact the first, Australian design was the Owen Gun, invented by a Lieutenant Evelyn Owen of the Australian Army. A limited run of 100, in various calibres, was made up for trial in the autumn of 1940 and as a result of these trials the model in 9-mm Parabellum was selected for service in 1941.

The Owen looks distinctly odd when compared to other submachine-guns. In the first place, the magazine was on top, feeding by gravity and spring power, very much like the original Vilar Perosa. It had a spidery and angular look to it and, to crown it all, it was usually painted brown and green camouflage colours, unlike any other gun before or since. But it all made sense. The top mounted magazine was extremely reliable, and the Owen never suffered from stoppages as did the Sten or Austen. On the other hand the top magazine made the gun rather more conspicuous, hence the jungle camouflage. An unusual mechanical detail was that the body held an internal stop ring to limit the rearward movement of the bolt. Since this was fixed inside the receiver, the bolt could not be withdrawn backwards through the rear end, as in most submachine-guns, and so the barrel had to be fitted with a quick-release plunger so that it could be pulled out of the receiver front end to allow the bolt to be withdrawn forward for cleaning.

The design called for a lot of careful machining, so that the production never reached astronomical figures – 45,000 were made before production stopped in September 1944 – and it was generally admitted to be somewhat heavier than was desirable. But in spite of that, it was one of the most popular submachine-guns ever made. The Australian troops in the Far East swore by it, as did British and Americans who had the opportunity to use it. It remained in service with the Australian Army until 1962.

By 1941 the US Army was looking for a

submachine-gun to replace the Thompson, something which, like the British Sten, would be cheaper and easier to make. America being a gun-conscious country, there was no shortage of applicants coming forward with designs, most of which appeared to have been influenced by the Thompson. Some of the designs submitted were quite abysmal. One typical report of the period on a submitted submachine-gun said, 'The whole behavior of this weapon was so eccentric and erratic that it was difficult to assess the actual causes of the malfunctioning . . .', while another read, 'This carbine appears to be an undeveloped model of a poor design. Much work would have to be done before it could be made to work satisfactorily . . .'.

However, there were some good ones. One prominent American designer of automatic weapons was George Hyde, and he had been submitting various models for trial since 1934. Eventually, in 1942, a design of his

which had been built by the Inland Division of General Motors, and was therefore known as the Hyde-Inland gun, was approved for US Army use as the Submachine-gun M2. It was a simple blow-back weapon mounted into a wooden stock and using a bottom-feeding box magazine. It was, of course, in the US .45 auto pistol calibre. Tests showed it to be one of the most stable and accurate guns ever seen when fired at automatic.

Sub-Contractors
A contract was given to the Marlin Fire-arms Corporation to manufacture about 165,000 M2 guns, but they ran into considerable difficulties in setting up production. Sub-contractors failed them, specifications were not met, and the first production guns gave constant trouble when submitted for routine tests. Eventually the M3 gun went into production while the M2 was still struggling to get started, and in June 1943 the M2 was declared obsolete and aban-

doned, less than 400 having been made.

Marlin's problems with the M2 could not be blamed on lack of experience on their part, since they were, at that time, completing a contract for another submachine-gun, the United Defense Model 42. This had been designed prior to the war by Carl Swebilius of the High-Standard Manufacturing company, well-known for their target pistols, and was patented in October 1940. It was offered to the US Army in .45 calibre and favourably reported on, but at that time the simplified Thompson M1 was being perfected and the Army were unable to justify a second design. It was then demonstrated to the British and Dutch governments. The British considered that the design needed further development, but the Dutch were sufficiently impressed with it to order 15,000 guns in 9-mm Parabellum calibre. Marlin received the contract and produced the guns, but where they ever went to is a minor mystery of the war. Some certainly went to

United Defense UD M42 9-mm
Designed before the Second World War but not made until early 1942, the UD M42 appeared just as the Thompson went into large-scale production and hence only some 15,000 of these high-quality weapons were manufactured. Some were used by the OSS *Weight:* 9 lb 1 oz *Rate of fire:* 700 rpm *Muzzle velocity:* 1310 fps

Reising Model 50 .45-in
Developed as a Thompson replacement in 1940 and itself superseded by the M3, the Model 50 was however produced in some numbers, most of the output going to the US Marines. The mechanism was unduly complex even though it used a simple blow-back operation *Weight:* 6 lb 12 oz *Rate of fire:* 550 rpm *Muzzle velocity:* 920 fps

Java for the Dutch, before the Japanese invasion, and it is understood that some went via the SOE and OSS to various European resistance and partisan groups, but beyond that little is known.

Swinging Hammer

The UD M42 was a well-made weapon in its production form, operating in the usual blow-back system, though it is one of the select few in which the differential locking system was abandoned. The bolt was closed and stopped by the time the round was fired, the firing pin being operated by a swinging hammer which came into action by striking a fixed plate in the receiver as the bolt closed. Another unusual feature was a hold-open device operated by the magazine platform. This ensured that after the last shot in the magazine had been fired, the bolt was held back as an indication to the firer. A common enough feature in automatic pistols, this was rare in submachine-guns.

Another offering was the Reising sub-machine-gun, patented by Eugene C Reising in June 1940. Known as the Model 50, it was made by the Harrington & Richardson firearms company and was submitted for test to both the United States and the British Army. Neither were impressed by it, but it was adopted by the US Marine Corps, since they were desperate for a submachine-gun and were unable to obtain sufficient Thompsons because of the Army's priority orders. Small numbers were also supplied to Canada and to Russia, as well as to police forces and local defence units in the United States. A Model 55 was later produced, but this only differed from the Model 50 by having a folding wire butt and a pistol grip. Mechanically it was the same.

In action however it was a disaster; it was far too complicated, and the US Marines in the Pacific Theatre finished up throwing their Reisings into the nearest ditch. What the Russians must have thought of it, com-

pared to the spartan simplicity and reliability of their own weapons, would make chastening reading. Although it was a basic blow-back weapon, the matter was complicated by making it a delayed blow-back, in which the breech-bolt was locked at the instant of firing by having been forced up a ramp and into a recess in the roof of the receiver. Firing was by a cylindrical hammer striking a firing pin in the bolt. The weapon was cocked by reaching underneath the fore-end and pulling back a cocking handle concealed in the woodwork. Due to the close tolerances and clearance in the mechanism, any dirt entering the gun was practically guaranteed to jam it solid, and the conditions of warfare in the Pacific were not such as to bring out the best in the gun. On the other hand, as a police weapon operating in a less rigorous environment and with regular maintenance and cleaning, it was quite serviceable, and numbers of them are in use to this day.

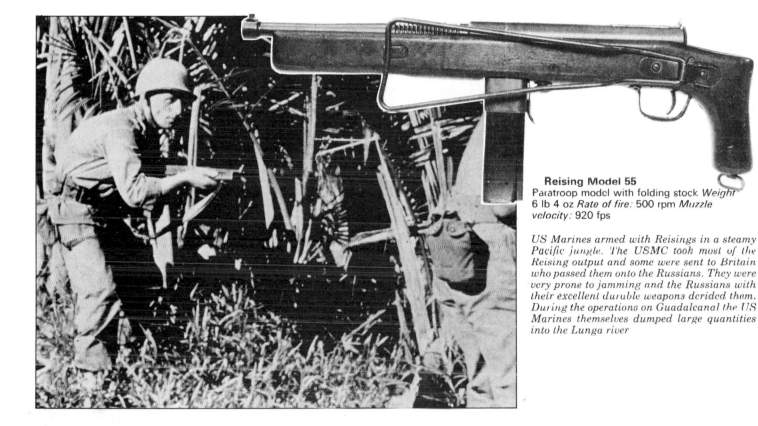

Reising Model 55
Paratroop model with folding stock *Weight:* 6 lb 4 oz *Rate of fire:* 500 rpm *Muzzle velocity:* 920 fps

US Marines armed with Reisings in a steamy Pacific jungle. The USMC took most of the Reising output and some were sent to Britain who passed them onto the Russians. They were very prone to jamming and the Russians with their excellent durable weapons derided them. During the operations on Guadalcanal the US Marines themselves dumped large quantities into the Lunga river

Hyde-Inland 45-in
Designed by George Hyde and built by Marlin, the M2 entered limited production in 1942 but the order was cancelled due to production difficulties after only some 400 had been made *Weight:* 9 lb 4 oz *Rate of fire:* 500 rpm *Muzzle velocity:* 960 fps

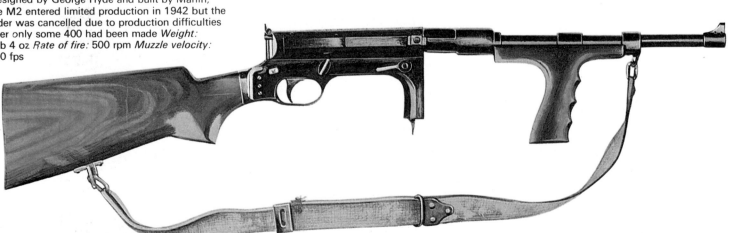

Eventually, after the disappointing response to their request for designs, the US Ordnance Department decided that their only hope was to design a gun themselves. The basic requirements were specified in February 1941, but time was wasted while the various weapons on offer from different designers and manufacturers were tried out. Finally design began in October 1942. The basic design came from George Hyde, and he was assisted by Frederick Sampson who, although not a firearms designer, was the Chief Engineer of the Inland Division of General Motors and highly skilled in production engineering. Between them, these two men developed the M3 submachine-gun, Hyde making sure that it would work and Sampson making sure that it could be stamped out by the million as cheaply as possible.

The gun was standardised for issue in December 1942, and production was undertaken by the Guide Lamp Division of General Motors in Anderson, Indiana, the first contract calling for 300,000 guns at $17.92 each, exclusive of the bolts which were made elsewhere. Most of the weapon was produced by stamping and pressing, only the bolt calling for any degree of precision machining.

The M3 was a simple blow-back gun which used a rather unusual crank mechanism for cocking the bolt. In 1944 reports began to come in of defects arising due to this cocking mechanism, and as a result a new design, the M3A1, was standardised in October 1944. In this version the cocking crank was done away with and cocking was performed by the simple expedient of the firer poking his finger into a hole in the bolt and pulling it back. A hinged cover over the cocking slot and ejection port had a spur welded to the inside, so that when the cover was closed the spur entered the cocking hole and locked the bolt in a safe condition.

One useful feature was that by changing the barrel and bolt and fitting an adapter into the magazine housing, the M3 could be changed from .45 ammunition to use 9-mm Parabellum ammunition, the adapter allowing the British Sten magazine to be used. Although thousands of these conversion kits were made, very few guns were ever converted, since there was always an ample

supply of .45 ammunition when the gun was in American hands, and people with 9-mm Parabellum ammunition were generally well-provided with Stens.

Silenced models of the M3 and M3A1 were also produced, in limited numbers, for use by Rangers and airborne troops, the silencer being based on that produced for the Sten gun. Since the .45 cartridge was subsonic, the design was less critical than that of the Sten and it appears to have been very effective.

In all, 622,163 M3 and M3A1 submachine-guns were made during the Second World War. At the beginning of the Korean War another contract for M3A1s was placed and a further 33,200 were made.

In the late summer of 1941 Germany invaded Russia and the Soviet Army was fighting for its life. With vast numbers of men being brought into the army, the training problem was enormous, and the simplicity of the submachine-gun made it the ideal weapon with which to arm such a mass army. Moreover, the submachine-gun suited the Soviet idea of tactics, with a submachine-gun you didn't hide in a hole and snipe, you had to get out and go for the enemy.

Left: Some M3s reached the British Army and by fitting an adapter and changing the barrel and bolt, Sten magazine and ammunition could be used, although this was not common practise. Right: The M3 in more familiar hands, with a US patrol in northern Alsace. The M3's shape quickly earned it the front-line epithet of 'Grease-Gun' and it did what it set out to do admirably – to be a cheap and reliable weapon which could be stamped out by the thousand in the shortest time possible

M3 .45-in
Simple, robust and cheap, the M3 was designed at Aberdeen Proving Ground and went further to meet the US Army's requirements for a mass-produced submachine-gun to supplement the Thompson than any of its private-entry rivals. It was passed for service at the end of 1942 and remained front-line equipment until 1960. The rate of fire was low making for steadiness and accuracy and its overall practicality was marred only by feed troubles with the magazine *Weight:* 8 lb 15 oz *Rate of fire:* 450 rpm *Muzzle velocity:* 900 fps

The Winter War of 1939–40 against the Finns had shown the utility of submachine-guns, in bitter and confused actions in the northern forests, where all the shooting was at short range and the quick response and high rate of fire of the submachine-gun paid off. The Finns were well-provided with the Suomi, and many battles in this war were fought almost entirely with these weapons. But the Degtyarev PPD-40 was not well suited to mass production, and a fresh designer, Georgii Shpagin, was asked to develop a new model which would be quicker and easier to make. In late 1940 he produced his design, and after extensive tests it was taken into use as the PPSh-41, just after the German invasion. In Russian terminology PP means 'Pistolet Pulyemet' or machine-pistol, and the following letter indicates the designer.

The construction of the PPSh was remarkably simple. The receiver and barrel jacket were stamped and formed from a single piece of steel, the bolt was a simple turning operation, the barrel could be made from half a standard rifle barrel, and the whole weapon was pinned and welded together in the simplest possible manner and mounted into a wooden stock. In spite of this, it was a sound weapon. The barrel was chromium

No propaganda picture of the wartime Russian soldier is complete without a submachine-gun and this seasoned veteran of the Red Army with his faithful PPSh-41 slung round his neck is no exception. The drum magazine held 71 rounds

plated internally to cut down wear and also to resist the adverse effects of hit-and-miss cleaning, which it was likely to get in action. The barrel jacket was extended in front of the muzzle to form a rudimentary form of compensator which, by directing some of the muzzle blast upwards, kept the muzzle down during automatic fire. The 71-round drum magazine of the PPD was adopted and, in addition, a 35-round box magazine was provided, though this was rarely seen in action.

The rate of fire was high at 900 rounds a minute, a result of the simple design and the powerful cartridge. Like all Soviet small-arms, the calibre was 7.62-mm, and the pistol cartridge developed a high velocity with a light bullet. In spite of the theoretical disadvantages of such a cartridge, the Russians used it throughout the war and for many years afterward, to good effect.

The PPSh became almost as much the badge of the Soviet soldier as the MP-38 was of the German, and no wartime propaganda picture was complete without one slung across the chest of a Red Army soldier. When production finally ended, shortly after the war, over five million had been made, and the design was widely copied in other Communist countries for several years afterwards.

The Soviet policy was, very wisely, to settle on a good design and then make it in quantity, ignoring any possible offers of replacement unless they promised considerable advantages. One gun for the war was their ideal; and yet circumstances brought one more Soviet submachine-gun into existence in 1942. In that year the German Army laid siege to Leningrad, and the stocks of arms in the city were insufficient to provide for all the able-bodied men and women who were preparing to man the barricades. A I Sudayev, an engineer in a Leningrad ammunition factory, designed a submachine-gun with which to arm these people, and his design was governed not by the tactical application of the weapon or any other of the standard military considerations, but simply by the two questions – what materials were available within the besieged city? And what machinery was available? The answers to those questions governed the design of the PPS-42 submachine-gun.

The PPS-42 is, except for two pieces of wood on the pistol grip and a scrap of leather inside the receiver acting as a bolt buffer, entirely of metal. The body of the receiver is stamped out of one sheet, the barrel jacket out of another, both were then bent and joined by rivets and spot-welding. The barrel was welded in place, a roughly turned bolt inserted, and a folding steel butt fitted. A 35-round box magazine was designed – since Sudayev had no machinery for making the drum magazines – and that was that. It fired only at automatic, at about 650 rounds a minute.

After the siege of Leningrad had been lifted the PPS continued in manufacture, a slightly modified version, the PPS-43, being produced. This was changed in minor details in the light of experience at Leningrad, the butt being slightly shorter, the safety catch made larger and easier to use, and the barrel given additional support. It continued in production until after the war, though not in such great numbers as the PPSh and it is estimated that about a million of both models of PPS were made.

Once the war ended they were removed

from Red Army service and given to various satellite nations. They turned up, for example, in Korea in 1952. It has been suggested that there was some political in-fighting behind this. The defenders of Leningrad were in some ways a political embarrassment for the Soviet leaders of the post-war years. If anyone was going to receive the nation's adulation, it was the Moscow hierarchy and not the upstarts from the North, and the whole Leningrad affair was played down for many years. This may have been the reason for disposing of the weapons which would always act as a reminder of the siege. Sudayev, moreover, does not appear to have been rewarded in any way, whereas Degtyarev and Shpagin were both made generals in the army, Doctors of technical science, heroes of Soviet Labour and showered with various other honours.

The PPS design, in fact, was the start of a very odd chain of events. In 1943 the Finns needed a submachine-gun which could be made faster than their old and well-tried Suomi, and since they were just across the border from Leningrad they managed to acquire a few PPS-42 models to study. The simplicity impressed them, and Willi Daugs, Chief Engineer of the Tikkakoski Arsenal, redesigned the weapon to take 9-mm Parabellum ammunition and put it into production as the Model 1944 for the Finnish Army. It is still in service there, a remarkable endurance record for what was originally intended as a cheap and desperate emergency design.

A Russian infantryman runs firing his PPSh-41 from the hip, a wounded German defender of Berlin is at his feet

PPS-42 7.62-mm

The PPS-42 was designed and produced in Leningrad during the seige of 1941–42. It is entirely stamped except for the barrel and bolt and spot welded together. The only non-metal parts are the wooden grips and a small piece of leather acting as a buffer for the bolt. Despite its crude appearance and poor finish it worked well. The magazine was a 35 round box. The gun saw action during the Korean war in 1951–52, but production was ceased in Russia in 1945 *Weight:* 7 lb 6 oz *Rate of fire:* 700 rpm *Muzzle velocity:* 1600 fps

PPS-42 action

PPSh-41 7.62-mm

Developed in 1940–41 as a replacement for the PPD-40 the Pisolet Pulyemet Shpagin became the trade mark of the Soviet soldier. It was a simple blow-back operated gun with a fixed firing pin and return spring and a crude firing mechanism. Its 71-round drum magazine gave it an edge over 32 round box magazine weapons like the MP 38 and it stood up well in the mud and snow of the Eastern Front. The gun could be turned out by semi-skilled labour and by the end of the war the Soviets had produced 5 million *Weight:* 8 lb *Rate of fire:* 900 rpm *Muzzle velocity:* 1600 fps

At the end of the war, Willi Daugs fled from the threat of a Russian occupation of Finland, and eventually surfaced in Spain, having taken the machine drawings of the Model 1944 gun with him as a sort of meal ticket. There he met another refugee, Ludwig Vorgrimmler, late of the Mauser company in Germany who was also travelling for his health, and the two of them ended up in the Oviedo Arsenal in Spain, making the Model 1944 again, this time as the DUX-51. About a thousand were made, and, among the customers were the West German border police who bought about a hundred. Daugs then went to Germany and collaborated with the Anschutz company of Ulm in improving the design, finally producing the DUX-59 model, which was basically the good old PPS but in a slightly better finish. After extensive tests the post-war German Army decided to adopt it. Daugs and Anschutz disagreed over licence rights and contract terms, and the DUX submachine-gun finally disappeared. But it is a remarkable sequence of events from humble beginnings.

The *Wehrmacht* however, while hanging on to the MP-38 and MP-40 designs, were always ready for more weapons and took several foreign guns into use during the war. At one stage they even went as far as modifying captured Soviet PPSh models to fire 9-mm ammunition. The simplicity of the Sten also attracted them and they built several near-copies of this weapon, principally for issue to their *Volkssturm* home guard units. One of the most remarkable

efforts was the *Gerät Potsdam* which was an absolutely identical copy of the Sten Mk 2 made by Mauser in conditions of great secrecy in late 1944. The copy was so exact that even the British inspector's stamps and proof marks were reproduced. The only way to detect the copy is by minute examination of the welds and dimensions of the parts. At a casual glance they appear to be genuine British models, and this is doubtless why, in spite of the fact that 25,000 were made, so very few remain today. Nobody realised that they were different.

A complaint from the German troops on the Eastern Front was that their MP-40s were fitted with a 32-round box magazine, whereas the Soviet troops opposed to them were armed with weapons mounting a 71-round drum magazine, which gave them an advantage during prolonged fire. The Erma company therefore devised a double-magazine mounting for the MP-40. This had a larger magazine housing and a sliding unit into which two standard 32-round magazines could be fitted side-by-side. The housing was then pulled across to one side, aligning one magazine with the bolt and barrel. The gun was fired in the normal way until the magazine was empty, when, after pulling back the bolt, the housing could be pushed across to bring the second magazine into play. An independent magazine catch for each magazine meant that the empty could now be removed, as opportunity offered, and replaced with a full one, though the gun was still capable of firing while the change was in progress.

Top: The British Mk 2 Sten (above) compared with the highly secret German copy codenamed 'Potsdam Device' and designed for clandestine operations. Above: The BV 1008, another Sten copy built by the famous engineering firm of Blohm and Voss but with no more sinister purpose other than to arm Volks-turm *units defending the crumbling Reich with a cheap Sten-type weapon*

Finnish M-44 9-mm
This is virtually a copy of the Soviet PPS-43 using 9-mm ammunition. A large number were made before 1944 by Oy Tikkakoski Ab and when the war ended the factory manager Willi Daugs moved to Sweden, thence to Holland and on to Spain. He took the drawings with him and the gun was subsequently made by Oviedo as the DUX SMG. It is a blow-back operated weapon with a 36 round box or 71 round drum magazine *Weight:* 6 lb 3 oz *Rate of fire:* 650 rpm *Muzzle Velocity:* 1310 fps

DUX 59 9-mm
The descent from the Soviet PPS-43 can easily be seen in the DUX design. The principal improvements, besides a better standard of manufacture and finish, are in the magazine housing, the safety catch, and in the provision of a tubular barrel jacket. It was a sound enough design, but politics and argument ruined its chances *Weight:* 6 lb 9 oz *Rate of fire:* 550 rpm *Muzzle velooity* 1200 fps

Left: Soviet Guards in Berlin armed with PPS-43s, the weapon born in desperation during the seige of Leningrad as the PPS-42, largely ignored by the Russians themselves yet copied in Finland and Spain as illustrated on this page

DUX 51
The Finnish M-44, itself a copy of the Soviet PPS-43, resurfaced postwar in Spain as the DUX-51 and the first customers ironically included the West German *Grenzpolizei*

One of the more inexplicable mysteries of the war is why the Japanese never made more use of submachine-guns. One would have thought that the submachine-gun would have been the ideal weapon for them, suiting their tactical doctrines perfectly. But they took very little interest in the submachine-gun until the mid-1930s, and not much more even then. A few SIG-made copies of the Bergmann MP-18 were bought by the Japanese Navy for their Marines in the late 1920s, but the Army made no move until about 1935. The Nambu company then began developing a gun in 8-mm calibre, the standard Japanese automatic pistol cartridge being used. Although tested by the Army they evinced no interest in it; it even got as far as Britain, being tested there in 1938 as a possible weapon for tank crews, but it was turned down. An improved model was then developed, but the idea was dropped for some time, then revived, and finally in 1940, the Model 100 appeared. Its acceptance by the military appears to have been due to the decision to form a force of airborne troops, for which lightweight weapons with high firepower were desirable.

In spite of the prolonged development period, the Model 100 appears to be nothing more than a slightly reorganised Bergmann, with wooden stock and perforated barrel jacket concealing a simple blow-back mechanism. A prominent bayonet bar is fitted to the front end of the barrel jacket, and some models had a simple form of compensator on the muzzle. There was also a variant model in which the butt was hinged to the stock so that it could be swung round to lie alongside the receiver and thus take up less space when carried. This was similar to the modification to the service rifle to suit it for airborne use.

In 1944 a revised model was introduced, the intention being to speed up manufacture. At last, it seems, the advantages of the submachine-gun in ordinary warfare were being recognised. External differences were small, the main one being that the bayonet bar was replaced by a smaller boss fitting, welded directly to the jacket. The front end of the jacket had a reduced-diameter extension formed into a compensator, the sights were simpler, and the whole gun was put together using rivets and welding. The return spring was made stiffer, increasing the rate of fire.

It has been estimated that no more than about 10,000 Model 100 guns, of both types, were made. They were used in the Japanese airborne attack on Java, but apart from that their appearance was rare.

While the combatant nations of the world were trying their hardest to produce submachine-guns which were ever more simple and ever more cheap, the neutral Swiss, naturally alarmed by the commotion beyond their borders, managed to produce the most expensive and complicated submachine-gun in history, a fact which deserves mention.

Swiss Precision
Early in 1940 the Swiss Army realised that there was an outside chance that they would have to defend their borders, and a stocktaking carried out as the Germans were sweeping through France disclosed that there were less than 500 serviceable submachine-guns in the country. What was more alarming was that the pistol ammunition stocks of the country were in 9-mm and 7.65-mm Parabellum, but only ten of the submachine-guns were chambered for either of these. The remainder were for odd things like 9-mm Mauser and 7.63-mm Mauser, stocks of which would be unlikely to last for more than a day or two of serious fighting. There was a quick decision taken,

Shikiki Kanshoju Type 100 8-mm
The Japanese troops that swept through the Pacific on a tide of conquest in 1942 were not lavishly equipped with submachine-guns – perhaps the ideal weapon for jungle fighting. A few Bergmann MP-28s were in service but the first native design – the Type 100, appeared in 1940 and only some 10,000 of the original model and 7500 of the folding butt parachutist's model had been made by 1943. In 1944 an improved model appeared eliminating some of the Type 100's defects, but again production of this simplified weapon was limited *Weight:* 8 lb 8 oz *Rate of fire:* 450 rpm *Muzzle velocity:* 110 fps

Furrer MP41 9-mm
Built with true Swiss precision, the MP41 was one of the most expensive submachine-guns ever made. It was however unnecessarily over-complex using a recoil-actuated toggle system rather like the Maxim principle. Rushed into production in 1940, the MP41's over complexity made it a military failure *Weight:* 11 lb 7 oz *Rate of fire:* 900 rpm *Muzzle velocity:* 1300 fps

and the weapons technical department ordered 100 guns from the government arsenal at Bern, and 50 guns from SIG.

SIG had, over the years, considerably modified their MKMO model. They had done away with the complicated two-piece bolt and adopted a simple blow-back action. The hinged magazine had been retained, though the weapon was made shorter so that it no longer resembled a rifle. It was a simple and sound design and SIG were ready to go into production. But for some unaccountable reason, the weapons technical staff turned down the SIG MP41 and adopted the weapon put forward by the Bern Arsenal. Since SIG could not sell the MP41 outside Switzerland due to their neutrality, that was the end of their hopes in that particular line, and no more than about 200 MP41s were ever made.

The weapon chosen for the Swiss Army was the Furrer MP41. Colonel Adolf Furrer was the designer for the Bern Arsenal, and his designs show that he was never a man to do things the easy way if there was a more difficult method of achieving his end. His guns are among the most complex ever made.

His MP41 was well up to standard in this respect, and it involved short recoil operation with a toggle lock, which in some respects resembles a Luger pistol laid on its side. The barrel slid back and forth in the jacket and in the receiver, and attached to the rear end was a 'barrel extension'. This barrel extension carried three hinged arms, the rearmost of which was anchored to a pivot in the receiver. Behind the barrel, of course, lay the bolt, and this had the front toggle arm pivoted to it. The third arm joined the other two, so that there was a linkage laid out along the barrel extension in a straight line behind the bolt when the gun was ready to fire. When it fired, the recoil of the case tried to open the bolt in the usual way, but the straight-line strut of the toggle arms prevented the bolt moving. Consequently the whole lot, barrel, bolt and extension, began to move back. As it did so, the rearmost arm, being attached to the body which was not moving, began to act on the toggle and eventually forced the straight-line to break sideways. This, in effect, destroyed the support behind the breech-block and allowed it to recoil. The barrel and extension was then stopped while the block carried on and performed the usual cycle of recoil and return, picking up a cartridge from the magazine and forcing it into the chamber. As the bolt closed, so the barrel moved forward again and the toggle straightened out to lock the bolt securely behind the chamber.

As might be imagined, the precise fit of the toggle was all-important, and the machining and fitting which had to be done was considerable. Moreover the action was clumsy, since a large casing had to be provided at the side of the receiver into which the toggle could move as the bolt opened. Nevertheless, it was accepted for service and went into production in January 1943. 4800 guns were produced in that year – and this was at a time when the Fazackerly factory was making 20,000 Sten guns *a week*.

The Swiss Army were less than delighted with their new weapon, and by the end of 1942, with the tooling-up for the MP41 going very slowly, they decided to look elsewhere. The Finns offered them the Suomi M1931 submachine-gun – which is strange, in view of the fact that the Finns were supposed to be at war at the time – and actually supplied 5000 guns to Switzerland in 1943. In the following year a licence was obtained and the Hispano-Suiza company set about making modified Suomis as the MP43/44.

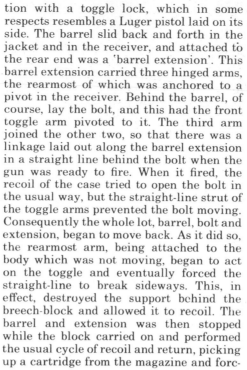

SIG MP41 9-mm
After making their MKMO model, SIG made a shorter version, the MKPO, for police use. Next, they dropped Kiraly's two-piece bolt and delayed action and adopted a simple blowback mechanism; incorporating this into the existing weapons turned them into the MKMS and MKPS models. In 1940, when the Swiss Army needed a submachine-gun, SIG made some small changes to the MKPS to produce their MP41. A pistol grip was added and the safety catch moved, but the folding magazine was retained and the 9-mm Parabellum cartridge adopted instead of the 9-mm Mauser. The result was an excellent weapon, but the Swiss test authority opted for the Furrer design instead. As a result, SIG turned to other things and no more than 200 of these guns were ever made *Weight:* 9 lb 10 oz *Rate of fire:* 850 rpm *Muzzle velocity:* 1300 fps

Swiss troops guard German prisoners who crossed the border into internment at the end of the war. Although the Swiss produced a succession of native designs, the troops themselves are armed with German MP-40s

Carl Gustav Model 45B
The 45B was introduced in 1950 and used either the 50 round Suomi magazine or the 36-round Carl Gustav magazine. The magazine housing is detachable

Carl Gustav M-45 9-mm
Appearing in 1945 after wartime development, the Swedish Kalspruta Pistol M-45 remains in production and service, and has seen extensive service with the Egyptian Army (it was built in Egypt as the 'Port Said') and in Indonesia *Weight:* 7 lb 9 oz *Rate of fire:* 600 rpm *Muzzle velocity:* 1250 fps

LOOKING FOR A WAR TO FIGHT

After the end of the Second World War in 1945, the armies of the principal contenders were well-equipped with submachine-guns. Economy and retrenchment were the watchwords of the day and little was done in the way of development within government circles. But the private gunmakers were well aware that sooner or later there would come a time when the existing stocks were run down or worn out and new designs would be wanted. Moreover there were several of the smaller countries, who had not been directly involved in the war, who had been cut off from the major gunmakers since 1939 and wanted to bring their military equipment up to date. So before the end of 1945, new designs of submachine-gun had begun to appear. Some were quite conventional but others were offering various novelties.

The first design to appear had, not surprisingly, been drawn up while the war was still in progress. The Swedish Army had been using the Suomi for several years, but in 1944 they decided that something new was needed, and the Carl Gustav Stads Gevarfactori of Eskilstuna, the official Swedish government arsenal, had set to work to produce a weapon better suited to mass production. The result was the Carl Gustav M-45 which has remained the standard Swedish submachine-gun since that time. It was sold widely to other countries, and, for a time in the 1950s, was made in Egypt as the 'Port Said' and formed the standard arm of the Egyptian Army.

The mechanism is largely derived from the Sten gun, a simple blow-back with differential locking. The body and jacket are of stamped steel, rivetted together, and a simple tubular butt, hinged to fold alongside the receiver, is used. In order to boost the performance, the Swedish Army developed an improved 9-mm Parabellum cartridge using a heavier bullet than normal, which is claimed to give better penetration.

Three variations of the M-45 exist. The original design was without a magazine housing, and accepted the standard 50-round Suomi box magazine, which was sensible in view of the number of such magazines the Swedish Army held. Then in the early 1950s the magazine design was changed for a new 36-round model. Either type of magazine could then be used, a removeable magazine housing being provided. This could be used to accept the 36-round magazine, or it could be slipped off the gun to allow the old 50-round magazine to be used. Shortly afterwards, when supplies of the new 36-round magazine were plentiful, the 50-round model was removed from service and all guns then had a permanently-attached magazine housing.

In the same year, the Madsen company of Denmark placed a submachine-gun on the market, the M/45. It was a most unusual design which can best be described as having been based on automatic pistol practice. The barrel was fixed to the frame of the gun, but instead of the usual fixed receiver with a bolt moving inside, the breech was closed by a light bolt which was pinned to an all-enveloping slide which covered the bolt and also enclosed the barrel. A return spring was around the barrel, pressing against the front end of the slide. To fire, the slide was gripped and pulled back, where it was held by the usual sort of sear mechanism. A magazine was inserted from below, again quite normal. When the trigger was pressed, however, the whole slide unit ran forward over the barrel, propelled by the internal spring, just the same as the slide of an automatic pistol. The bolt section pushed a cartridge into the breech. Inside the bolt was a firing pin, spring-loaded to stay *inside* the bolt – so that there was no danger of premature firing by a fixed pin should there be an obstruction to the cartridge entering the chamber. As the bolt came to rest against the base of the loaded cartridge, so a rotating hammer, flung up by a fixed block on the gun frame, drove the firing pin forward, overcoming the light spring loading, and firing the cartridge.

The Madsen M/45 was neat and tidy, but it was expensive to make, and it must have been disconcerting to have the top of the weapon suddenly lurch forward when the trigger was pressed. A few appear to have been sold to South America, but there was little other response to the design, and so the Madsen engineers went back to try again.

In 1946 they came back with a fresh design, and this time they had got it right. The M/46 was an instant success and sold in the hundreds of thousands around the world, until the Madsen company left the firearms business in the middle 1960s.

The method of operation is simple blow-back, but what makes the M/46 design unique is the method of construction. The receiver is in two pressed steel halves, hinged together at the rear end. The barrel drops into a groove at the front, the halves are closed like a book, and a barrel lock nut screws over the barrel to grip both halves and hold them securely. All the mechanical

May 1945, and the Danish resistance comes onto the streets of Copenhagen armed with Suomi M1931s hidden since 1940

BPC Picture Library

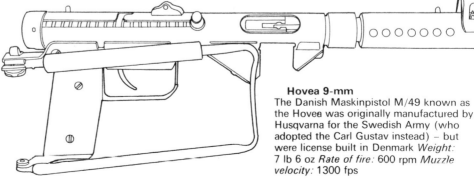

Hovea 9-mm
The Danish Maskinpistol M/49 known as the Hovea was originally manufactured by Husqvarna for the Swedish Army (who adopted the Carl Gustav instead) – but were license built in Denmark *Weight:* 7 lb 6 oz *Rate of fire:* 600 rpm *Muzzle velocity:* 1300 fps

parts are attached to the right-hand side of the receiver so that, in effect, the left side is merely the lid of the box. Repair and replacement of parts is simple, and cleaning could not be easier, provided some care is taken not to lose any of the pieces when the gun is opened.

The 1946 model can be recognised by the cocking handle, which is a flat plate on top of the receiver with flanges at the sides which can be gripped in the fingers for pulling back. The 1950 model uses a more normal cocking knob which protrudes through a slot in the top of the receiver. In 1953 a change was made in the magazine, a curved model being adopted instead of a straight one, but the biggest change lay in the method of assembly. The barrel lock nut no longer screwed on to the receiver to hold the two halves together; instead, the barrel was made with a flange which engaged in recesses inside the receiver. The lock nut

screwed onto a section of thread on the barrel and, working against the front of the receiver, it pulled the barrel tightly into the internal bearings in the receiver and locked everything solid.

The Model 50 came along just as the British Army were contemplating replacing the Sten gun with something better, and it was tested in 1950. The results were so good that for a short time it was expected that it would be adopted by the British Army, but it was not. There were also other contenders.

Although the Sten had served the British Army well, it never shook off the 'cheap and desperate' image. Names like the 'Woolworth Gun', the 'Stench Gun' and others even worse were freely used. The final version, the Mk 5, went some way towards 'traditional' appearance and finish, by using a wooden butt and pistol grip, and shaping the muzzle in the same manner as a Lee-Enfield rifle so that the service bayonet

could be fitted. But whatever was done to the Sten, nothing was ever done to the magazine, however, and the last model was no better than the first when it came back to the basic question of reliability.

During the war a number of new designs had been put forward, but, rightly, the official attitude was that the Sten was serving well enough and refinements could wait until there were less pressing matters of importance for the armament industry to attend to. Once the war was over, though, a Sten replacement was high on the list of priorities.

The Lanchester submachine-gun had been made by the Sterling Engineering company of Dagenham, and following its production Mr Patchett, the designer for Sterling, had spent some time improving the design, submitting his improved models from time to time. These were always tried, but were generally found wanting in some respect.

Patchett
Silencer Construction Breakdown

Patchett
Silencer showing baffles

Hotchkiss Mitraillette 9-mm
Called the 'Type Universel' and originally designed in 1949 for the French police, this over-complicated weapon was not adopted by the French Army
Weight: 7 lb 8 oz *Rate of Fire:* 650 rpm *Muzzle velocity:* 1300 fps

Broadly speaking, they simply were not quite good enough to justify putting the Sten out of production.

In January 1944 the General Staff issued a set of specifications to which any new submachine-gun would have to conform. Basically, this demanded a weapon in 9-mm calibre, weighing not more than 6 lb, firing at a rate not exceeding 500 rounds a minute, and capable of putting five single shots into a foot square at 100 yards range. To meet this specification, Mr Patchett submitted a new model. The Army were sufficiently impressed with it to order 20 guns for trials in April 1944. Trials were carried out and the Ordnance Board reported that they, 'considered the Patchett machine-carbine suitable for service'. In fact, some of those original 20 guns went to Arnhem with the airborne troops later in the year.

In the postwar lull there was little interest shown in the Patchett for some time. During this time a variety of designs were put forward by the Design Department at Enfield, but none of them progressed beyond the prototype stage. In 1947, however, interest in the submachine-gun again revived and a comparative trial was organised. Into this went the latest Patchett, an Enfield design, an Australian experimental model, a Sten (as comparison) and a new design from the Birmingham Small Arms company. This BSA weapon was very neat in design with an unusual system of cocking in which the plastic fore-end was gripped and pushed forward over the muzzle, a system which meant that to recock the gun in the event of a stoppage the firer had no need to change his grip.

The trial was somewhat inconclusive, all the weapons displaying faults of one sort or another, and it was followed by a period of development and more trials. Finally, in 1951, the Patchett had demonstrated its superiority to all the competing designs and it was selected to be the replacement for the Sten. Although it was always referred to during development as the Patchett, following its adoption by the Army it has always been known as the Sterling, after the maker's name. The official name is, of course, something else again – Sub Machine-Gun L2A1.

The Sterling operates in the usual blow-back mode, but it incorporates some ingenious features. The bolt, for example, is made with sharp grooves on its outer surface, which act as a self-cleaning device and cut away any dirt or dust which may enter the receiver. The magazine follower, which pushes the cartridges, is fitted with rollers to reduce friction and give a positive and non-jamming feed. The butt collapses and folds very compactly, and the internal design is such that the firing pin does not line up with the cartridge cap until the

Patchett Mk 1 9-mm
The first Patchett submachine-gun was demonstrated in September 1942. After some modifications, 120 were produced for troop trials in 1944, and several of these trial models were used by airborne troops in the Battle of Arnhem, later that year. An important feature was the incorporation of anti-fouling grooves in the bolt, which swept out dirt as the gun was fired. Even so, it was to be another nine years before the design was adopted for service. *Weight:* 6 lb 4 oz *Rate of fire:* 600 rpm *Muzzle velocity:* 1250 fps

A British soldier takes careful aim with his Sterling L2A1, the standard submachine-gun of the British armed services since 1954

MOD

cartridge has actually entered the chamber, giving a high degree of safety in operation.

In Europe, new designs of several sub-machine-gun appeared after the war. The French Army began re-equipping itself after the war. The MAS-38 had continued in production throughout the war, and there were a variety of submachine-guns obtained from the Allies and also from Germany as reparations, but it was obviously desirable to scrap them all and adopt a standard model. The chosen model was the MAT-49, developed by the Manufacture d'Armes National de Tulle and adopted by the French Army in 1949. It was a simple and orthodox blow-back design, the body being rectangular in section and put together from heavy steel stampings. The only novel feature was that the magazine could be folded forward to lie beneath the barrel. The wire stock could be telescoped into the receiver, and with both these actions completed, the MAT folded up into a very small package, convenient for carrying. As well as being adopted by the Army, the MAT is frequently seen in the hands of French police.

The Manufacture d'Armes National de Tulle also featured in the dubious history of a Swiss submachine-gun, the Rexim-Favor. This weapon was an entertaining example of what happens when people take a flyer into firearms design without thinking the thing through. The Rexim company was formed in Switzerland in 1951 to promote a submachine-gun designed by Colonel Favier. (According to some sources, the design was actually French, and had been stolen from the Tulle factory by a beautiful female spy!)

The manufacture of the gun was contracted to a Spanish factory for manufacture in 1953, and 5000 were made. A few more were sent to Switzerland as sales samples, and the Rexim agents began promoting the gun in various countries. They had no succuss, however, and in 1957 the Rexim company went bankrupt. This left the Spanish firm with the better part of 5000 guns on their hands. They made the best of it by rechristening them the 'La Coruna', but they had no better success, and it was not adopted as a service weapon by any nation. In the end, it seems, the stock was sold off to anyone who wanted submachine-guns desperately enough, and some were later to appear in trouble spots such as Nigeria and the Congo. Doubtless there are

A Vietnamese soldier in the French Army armed with a MAT-49 brings in a VietMinh prisoner

Topham/Keystone

MAT-49 9-mm
Tested in the Indo-Chinese War and Algeria the MAT-49 is a very solid and ingeniously designed gun with a 32 round box magazine. The magazine pivots forward when not in use to lock beneath the barrel, while the butt telescopes forward to reduce the guns length from 28 ins to 22. It has a grip safety, which with the magazine secured forward makes it a very safe weapon. The 'wrap round bolt' similar to the Uzi keeps the working parts compact *Weight:* 8 lb *Rate of fire:* 600 rpm *Muzzle velocity:* 1150 fps

still some about the world awaiting their chance.

What sank the Rexim as much as anything else was its complex and unnecessary design features. It fired from a closed bolt, thus almost guaranteeing trouble from cook-offs, and yet it was a blow-back weapon with no form of delay device. The bolt carried a floating pin and was pushed by a strong return spring. Around this went another spring which acted on a tubular hammer. When the weapon was cocked, both units, hammer and bolt, were pulled back, and when the cocking lever was released the bolt ran forward to chamber the cartridge but the hammer was held back by the sear. On pulling the trigger, the sear released the hammer which then went forward to strike a cross-bar in the back of the bolt and drive the firing pin forward. The recoiling bolt then had to overcome its own return spring and also push the hammer back against the hammer spring on its travel to the rear.

Several options were available to prospective purchasers, in the way of barrels of varying lengths, different sizes of magazine, bayonets, even a grenade launcher to fit on the muzzle. All to no avail. The moral is perhaps that if you must steal a design to go into business, make sure you steal a good one.

The war had introduced the submachine-gun to many people who had not given it a thought before. As a result, many of them decided that there was a future in weapons design and manufacture, though several of them went into the business without stopping to consider who was going to buy their products. The postwar years saw a plentiful supply of war-surplus submachine-guns on the market, and a design had to be either very good, very cheap, or capable of being supplied in very large numbers in order to compete. Few met this requirement.

One of the few which managed to survive was the Ingram submachine gun. Gordon Ingram served during the war and returned to the USA intent upon making a sub-machine-gun for police use. In 1946 he produced his 'Model 5', so-called because the Army had already standardised their M1, M2 and M3 and were contemplating an M4. The Model 5 was a very simple design with the receiver and jacket made of seamless steel tubing, and with only three moving parts – the trigger, sear and bolt. Fitted with a wooden butt, had a 25-round magazine, weighed just over 6 lb and was a simple and robust weapon. But in 1946 nobody was particularly interested, and the Model 5 never went past the prototype stage.

Nothing daunted, Ingram set to work to produce a new design, and in 1949 came the Model 6, which was put on the market by the Police Ordnance company, formed by Ingram and three friends. Like so many other American designs, the Model 6 showed lingering traces of the Thompson influence, with forward pistol grip, finned barrel and wooden butt. It was, however, a much simpler weapon than the Thompson. The mechanism was the usual blow-back with differential locking and the gun was offered in .45, .38 ACP and 9-mm chambering. The Model 6 was demonstrated at the California Police Chief's Convention in 1949 and subsequently sold in some numbers. As well as several thousand sold in the USA it was bought by the Peruvian government for their army and was later built in Peru.

The Model 6 was originally designed to fire only at automatic. A later model, still

Imp .221-in
Commissioned by the USAF as a 'survival weapon' the tiny Imp was developed by Colt in the late sixties and is designed so that the firer's forearm should act in place of a butt. Two examples were tested in Vietnam and although able to fire single or full automatic the Imp is classified as a rifle *Weight:* 4 lb *Rate of fire:* 500 rpm *Muzzle velocity:* 2400 fps

Ingram Model 10 and 11
These are similar weapons differing only in weight and length due to the ammunition used. The guns are small (10.5-ins and 8.75-ins) and light (loaded with 30 and 32 rounds respectively they weigh 8.40 lb and 4.17 lb) which makes them ideal weapons for guards and security men. They have been sold to Chile and Yugoslavia and trial batches have been evaluated by many countries *Weight:* 6.25 lb and 3.5 lb *Rate of fire:* M10 .45 ACP 1145 rpm, M10 1090 rpm, M11 1200 rpm *Muzzle velocity:* M10 .45 ACP 920 fps, M10 1200 fps, M11 960 fps
(The examples shown are fitted with silencers)

numbered 6, had a trigger mechanism which allowed single shots when the trigger was pulled back one stage, automatic fire when it was pulled fully back. But Ingram then developed the Model 7 which used a two-part bolt and a separate firing pin to permit single shot firing from the closed bolt position, since much of the police work required accurate single shots.

The Model 7, however, never went into production, and in 1952 the Police Ordnance company was wound up. Ingram then went Thailand, where he spent some time setting up production facilities for a Model 8, which was little more than a slightly improved Model 6 having improved safety devices. Later, after his return to the USA, he developed a Model 9, which was simply a Model 8 with a sliding wire butt, though, again, this never went into production.

In 1969 Ingram went to work for a company called Sionics Incorporated, who, in 1970, expanded their activities and became the Military Armaments Corporation. Here he produced two models based on a completely fresh design, the Models 10 and 11. There was very little difference between the two, the M10 being produced in .45 and 9-mm calibres and the M11 in 9-mm Short or .380. The .380 cartridge has rarely been used in submachine-guns, being less powerful and shorter than the 9-mm Parabellum cartridge, but as a result the M11 is considerably smaller and lighter than the M10 model.

Both weapons were simple and robust steel pressings, with a magazine fitting into the pistol grip and a sliding wire stock. The design was extremely compact, commending it to vehicle crews, mortar crews and other soldiers whose prime concern was other work and who wanted a sidearm which would be in their way as little as possible.

The most unusual feature of these two guns was the provision of a screwed section on the barrel, just in front of the receiver. This was designed to accept a silencer or, as MAC called it, a 'suppressor'. This was a standard item of supply with the Ingrams, largely because MAC, in their Sionics days, were principally concerned with the production of weapon suppressors.

The Ingram suppressor worked in a different way from the usual run of Maxim-type silencers for firearms, which is doubtless why the company were careful to refer to it as a 'suppressor' rather than as a silencer. In the first place, contrary to other submachine-gun silencers, it did not reduce the bullet velocity and therefore a super-sonic bullet could still be heard as it passed through the air. But it did muffle the report of the gun so as to make it difficult to discover the location of the firer. Several thousand M10 and M11 models with the MAC suppressor were made and they were adopted by Chile and Jugoslavia, as well as being evaluated by several other countries.

The compactness of the Ingram – the Model 10 is only 10½-in long with the butt collapsed – is due to the development of what is known variously as the 'wrap-around', or 'overhung', or 'telescoping' bolt. To understand the significance of this, it is necessary to go back to the war years.

119

One of the fundamental factors in submachine-gun design was the simple physical demand for sufficient room for the bolt to recoil and complete the firing cycle. Where the bolt was a simple cylinder of steel, confined in diameter by the size of the gun's receiver, it meant that to obtain the necessary weight, it had to be five or six inches long. It had to have sufficient room to move back, compressing the return spring behind it, until it cleared the magazine and ejection ports. If the bolt had been made too light, in an attempt to shorten it, then the reduction in mass meant a much higher rate of fire, one which might well be too great for control. To take the earliest example, the Bergmann MP-18, the bolt weighed 25 oz and travelled 3.5 in back on firing. Allowing some space for the coils of the return spring, this means a receiver, behind the breech, at least 10-in long. Add this to the length of the barrel and you are arriving at a sizeable weapon.

But by the middle of the war it was apparent that the submachine-gun needed to be a compact weapon, something easily carried inside a vehicle or by a parachutist, and not something resembling a fully-stocked rifle. Some basic thinking had to be done, and so far as can be ascertained the first man to hit on the answer was an Italian designer named Giovanni Oliani who worked for the Fabricca de Armas de Guerra of Cremona. In 1942 he produced a prototype submachine-gun which broke new ground by using the overhung bolt for the first time.

The overhung bolt can best be described as follows. An ordinary bolt is made, somewhat oversize, and then a deep hole is drilled into the face. At the bottom of this hole a new bolt face and firing pin is made. The barrel is then mounted within the receiver so that it sticks into the receiver as an unsupported tube. Then, when the bolt goes forward, the breech end of the barrel will enter the hole in the bolt until the new bolt face reaches the breech. At that point, with the bolt closed, there is more of the bolt overhanging the barrel than there is behind it, so that although the necessary weight is there, the actual amount of bolt behind the breech is very small – just sufficient to withstand the explosion and carry the firing pin – and the amount of recoil travel is correspondingly reduced.

There are obvious complications. Slots and holes would have to be cut into the bolt in order to permit feed and ejection, though

it has been done. A simpler way is that adopted by Oliani, who made a bolt which resembled a letter 'L' laid on its face. The actual bolt was very short, but attached above it was a large length of steel which stretched forward over the barrel when the bolt was closed. This meant that a metal casing had to be made above the barrel into which this overhung section could pass. One advantage of making the bolt so short was that the balance of the weapon changed less as it was fired. The bolt also travelled a shorter distance, and the pistol grip could be brought more central until it actually surrounded the magazine. This brought another advantage. Changing a sub-machine-gun magazine in the dark was a

chancy business, with the firer often fumbling around to try and find the magazine housing with the end of the fresh magazine. But where the magazine went into the pistol grip, magazine changing in the dark became simple, for the basic human reason that one hand can rapidly find the other, even in pitch darkness, and since one hand was wrapped around what was, in effect, the magazine housing, the other hand knew instinctively where to place the magazine.

In spite of all this brilliant innovation, Oliani got nowhere with his prototype 'OG42' gun, and it has long since vanished. But in 1944 he developed another, the OG44 and two specimens of this have survived. He still used the overhung bolt, though he

A platoon of Israeli paratroopers all armed with Uzis

Uzi 9-mm
Developed by Major Uziel Gal of the Israeli Army, the Uzi is in service with Israel, West Germany, Iran, South Africa and Venezuela. It is a compact weapon which measures 18.5 ins with the butt folded, and includes a combined pistol grip and magazine housing which simplifies loading at night. The Uzi is made from a wide range of stampings and weldings. It has a 25 round magazine and adjustable sights set at 100 and 200 metres *Weight*: 8 lb *Rate of fire*: 550–600 rpm *Muzzle velocity*: 1312 fps

Armaguerra OG-44 9-mm
This little-known prototype was one of the first designs ever to use the 'overhung' bolt, but it unfortunately appeared in 1944, a time when few people were in the market for submachine-guns. Only two specimens are known to have survived, this one and another with a folding steel butt
Weight: 6 lb 12 oz *Rate of fire:* 525 rpm *Muzzle velocity:* 1350 fps

abandoned the pistol grip magazine housing. He did, though, introduce another useful feature which has since been widely copied – the use of a grip safety lock on the pistol grip itself. This was a plate at the back of the grip linked to a bolt-locking mechanism. Unless the pistol grip was held correctly and the plate squeezed in, the bolt could not be freed, so that accidental firing by dropping the weapon was quite impossible. But again, Oliani had no luck; 1944 was no time to be introducing new submachine-guns, and he was unable to interest anyone in production.

The first production submachine-gun to use the overhung bolt appeared in Czecho slovakia in 1948, designed by Vaclav Holek, the man who had designed the prototype of the famous Bren light machine-gun. Whether Holek knew of Oliani's pioneering work with the overhung bolt is open to question. It seems unlikely, and the idea is so basic that there is no reason why it should not have occurred to Holek quite independently. But the Ceskoslovenska Zbrojovka armaments factory had a high reputation for arms design and were anxious to get back into the world markets after the war. They were thus ready to back Holek's judgement to a greater degree than the Cremona factory had been prepared to back Oliani.

The CZ23 was a simple and compact weapon, the receiver being a steel tube with the barrel protruding inside it for some distance. The bolt was 8.25 in long, but was hollowed out so that when closed 6.25 in of its length were wrapped around the barrel. Slots for feed and ejection were cut in the bolt, and the design was so arranged that the ejection ports in the bolt and in the receiver only coincided during the bolt's travel, as the cartridge case was ready to be ejected. At all other times, when the bolt was either closed or open, the ports did not coincide and thus no dirt could enter the mechanism. Another interesting mechanical feature was the system of firing. For single shots the trigger was pressed lightly, for automatic fire it was pressed more strongly, against a safety spring.

The model 23 was fitted with a wooden stock. A model 25 was also produced, having a folding metal stock but otherwise exactly the same. Production began in 1949 and the gun was issued to the Czech Army, but in 1952 the Soviets insisted on the use of their standard 7.62-mm ammunition by their satellites, and the 9-mm CZ guns were withdrawn to be replaced by the Models 24 and 26. These were exactly the same as the 23 and 25 but chambered for the Soviet 7.62-mm cartridge. The 9-mm models were then sold off to various countries, notably Syria and Cuba.

The CZ models brought the idea of the overhung bolt into prominence, and they were a considerable influence on future designs. One of the most important of those, and probably the best-known, is the Uzi submachine-gun, made in Israel.

The Uzi was one of the first military products to appear after the foundation of Israel. One reason for its early arrival was that in the 1948 Arab-Israeli war the Israelis had few submachine-guns and felt the lack of them in the type of fighting involved. In 1949 Major Uziel Gal of the Israeli Army began work on a submachine-gun design, and the resulting weapon, the Uzi (derived from Gal's name) was introduced in 1951. It has since been widely adopted in other countries. As well as being made in Israel it has been made under licence by Fabrique National of Liège in Belgium, one of whose products is a folding-butt version of the Uzi, used by the West German Army as their Maschinen Pistole 2.

The most striking feature of the Uzi is its compact shape and small size when compared to most of the designs which preceded it, and this compactness was due to the use of an overhung bolt. This is square in section and hollowed out at the front to wrap around the barrel for 3.75 in, allowing the barrel to be set back into the receiver. So that within an overall length of 18.5 in, the Uzi has a 10.5-in barrel. Arising from this mid-position of the breech, the Uzi magazine goes into the pistol grip, giving excellent support to the magazine and placing the centre of balance of the gun over the grip so that it is possible to fire it one-handed. Construction is largely of steel pressings, and tolerances within the receiver are liberal so that the Uzi is not upset by operating in dirty or dusty surroundings. Taken all round, the Uzi has turned out to be one of the classic designs, one which is likely to see service for several years.

In Italy, the birthplace of the overhung bolt, little notice was taken of it for some years. The Beretta company continued to produce slight modifications of the Model 38A until the early 1950s. But in 1957 Tullio Marengoni retired and his place was taken by Domenico Salza. Salza had, in 1952, begun design studies into a new submachine-gun, his principal aims being economical manufacture allied with simplicity and strength, plus accuracy and controllability. To achieve this he took to the overhung bolt as a method of keeping the centre of balance of the gun low, and adopted stamped steel as his construction material instead of the expensively machined products which Beretta had previously made.

During 1954–58 Salza produced a number of prototypes before producing, in 1958, the

Erma MP-58 9-mm
The Erma company had designed the famous German MP-38 and MP-40, and this postwar design still shows evidence of its parentage. The tubular receiver, barrel locking nut, magazine housing and pistol grip are recognisably derived from the MP-40, and the mechanism used the Vollmer telescoping mainspring and bolt unit. The MP-58 was tested by the Bundeswehr in 1959 but was not adopted for service *Weight:* 6 lb 10 oz *Rate of fire:* 700 rpm *Muzzle velocity:* 1250 fps

Beretta Model 12, which was quite obviously a break with the previous family of Beretta weapons. It was adopted by the Italian Army as the M12 for use by special service troops. Numbers were then sold to Saudi Arabia, and it is still manufactured under licence in Indonesia.

The Model 12 is made very simply, of metal pressings welded together. The pistol grip, magazine housing, fore-grip and receiver are one solid unit. The bolt is of the overhung type, tubular and with about 6 in of its length surrounding the barrel when closed. A folding butt lies alongside the receiver when not in use, or a wooden butt can be provided. An interesting addition is a grip safety in the forward edge of the pistol grip, below the trigger guard. Unless this is firmly gripped and forced inward, the bolt remains locked against any movement. There is also a conventional push-button safety catch above the trigger.

Strangely, the Czechs, having originated the overhung bolt, abandoned it for their next submachine-gun, a most odd weapon which goes by the name of the 'Skorpion'. This is so small as to be more in the nature of a machine-pistol. It fires the .32 automatic pistol cartridge, the only submachine-gun to do so, and a cartridge which is not generally considered to be a combat-worthy round. But the object of the tiny Skorpion is to provide tank and armoured car crews in the Czech Army with personal protection which can be holstered on the belt, as a pistol, and fired one-handed if necessary, while at the same time providing them with a weapon which can be used for covering fire around their vehicle up to a range of 200 yards or so in order to keep an enemy occupied until the tank or armoured car's machine-gun can be brought into play.

The Skorpion is tiny; 10.65-in long with the wire stock retracted, and less than 3 lb in weight. The small bolt is quite conventional and operation is blow-back, though firing is done by a hammer mechanism. Such a small bolt would, in the normal way, lead to a very high and uncontrollable rate of fire, but the Skorpion incorporates a 'rate retarder'. As the bolt goes to the rear, it drives a weight down into the hollow pistol grip against the pressure of a spring, and at the same time the bolt is held back by a trip-catch. The weight is rebounded from the

bottom of the pistol grip by its spring, flies up and releases the trip-catch to allow the bolt to go forward to chamber the next cartridge and trip the hammer. In this way a very slight delay is introduced into the bolt movement, which brings the rate of fire down to about 650 rounds a minute, which is, in this calibre, controllable.

Since its introduction, some variant models of the Skorpion have appeared, differing in the ammunition they use. As might be expected, the .32 round has been replaced by 9-mm chamberings, the first being the Soviet 9-mm Makarov automatic pistol cartridge. This is rather larger and more powerful than the 9-mm Short or .380 pistol round, though still less powerful than the 9-mm Parabellum. It can be taken as being the upper limit of power possible in a straight blow-back weapon without any form of differential or other locking. In 1968, a new Skorpion with 9-mm Parabellum chambering was produced. This, naturally enough, was larger and more robust than the original model, but the system of operation remains the same.

And so, back to the place where it all began – Germany. When the West German Army came into being, there were several submachine-gun designs on offer from German makers. Among the contenders was the Erma company. Their original factory at Erfurt had been overrun by the Russian Army and had vanished into the East German People's Republic, but the key staff and technicians had managed to escape and, eventually, the factory was set up afresh in Dachau, Bavaria. In 1955 they came back into the submachine-gun business by attempting to promote a French design which used a peculiar crank and flywheel mechanism to control the bolt. It was a hopeless proposition, and it seems that Erma simply took it on as a technical exercise for their engineers. They certainly never had any success in selling it. They then sat down and produced several designs of their own, which need not be covered in detail, until in 1959, at the German Army's request for something cheap and effective, they developed their MP-58.

This was, in fact, little more than a return to their successful MP-38 design. The same telescoping bolt assembly that Vollmer patented was used, the same corrugated

magazine housing and magazine, the same pistol grip and barrel retaining nut. All that had changed was the receiver, no longer in a plastic body, and the folding stock, which became a simple piece of bent wire which folded over the top of the gun. The only major mechanical change was the incorporation of a buffer at the rear of the receiver which cushioned the return of the bolt and thus slowed down the rate of fire to the 600 rpm the Army wanted. However, by the time the gun was ready for testing, the departmental heads in the Army had changed, new specifications had been issued, and the MP-58 was no longer acceptable.

In 1960 Erma came back again with a new design, quite different from anything they had produced before. Receiver and jacket were stamped from a single piece of steel, the Vollmer bolt was abandoned for a rectangular bolt having two guide rods and return springs through it, the stock folded sideways and the magazine was the Swedish Carl Gustav type. Forty hand-built weapons were made and delivered to the Army for testing, but no orders were placed. Erma then set to work to make improvements, but while they were doing this, the German Army decided to adopt the Uzi. At that, Erma gave up the submachine-gun business as a bad job.

The only other German company to get anywhere with a submachine-gun design in recent years has been the Heckler & Koch company of Oberndorf. This firm came into prominence in the postwar years by producing the G3 service automatic rifle which was used to arm the West German Army, the Portuguese Army, and later the armies of about thirty other countries. In the mid-1960s the company developed a submachine-gun called the MP-5 which is, in many respects, no more than a cut-down edition of the G3 rifle. It uses the same delayed blow-back mechanism, receiver, trigger, pistol grip and stock assemblies, a standardisation which doubtless contributes to manufacturing efficiency and economy.

The delayed blow-back system of the MP-5 relies upon a two-piece bolt which, when closed, presses two rollers into recesses in the sides of the receiver. The HK MP-5 is also unusual in firing from a closed bolt by means of a hammer striking a firing pin, this feature stemming from its rifle parentage.

Heckler & Koch MP 5 9-mm
Derived from a successful rifle and using the same type of roller-locked delayed blow-back operation allowing accurate fire from a closed-bolt, the MP 5 is simply made of sheet stampings and plastic furniture. The MP 5A2 has a permanent plastic stock and the MP 5A3 a telescopic metal stock (MP 5A2) *Weight:* 5 lb 6 oz *Rate of fire:* 650 rpm *Muzzle velocity:* 1312 fps

Beretta Model 12 9-mm
The Model 12 is the latest in a line of SMGs developed by Beretta since the war. It includes a grip safety which can be secured by a button on the left of the rear grip. Like most modern SMGs it has a wrap round bolt and is made from stampings and brazings, but despite these time and cost saving features it performs well. It has been bought by Brazil, Gabon, Libya, Nigeria, Saudi Arabia and Venezuela and manufactured by Bandung Arsenal, Indonesia *Weight:* 6 lb 10 oz *Rate of fire:* 550 rpm *Muzzle velocity:* 1250 fps

Skorpion VZ/61 7.65-mm
A machine-pistol rather than a true submachine-gun, the Czech Skorpion was originally conceived as a holster weapon for AFV crews and is small enough to be fired in single-shots from one hand. Although a simple blow-back weapon, an inertia device slows down the rate of fire *Weight:* 2 lb 14 oz *Rate of fire:* 700 rpm *Muzzle velocity:* 975 fps

When the cartridge fires, the pressure forces the bolt head rearwards, but the movement can not be transferred to the bolt body until the rollers have been forced out of their recesses. This happens quite quickly, but there is sufficient delay to allow the bullet to leave the short barrel and for the breech pressure to drop before the bolt body begins to move.

The MP-5 is a selective fire-weapon, but there is an interesting option available, a burst-fire regulator. This is a ratchet device in the trigger mechanism which allows from two to five rounds, as selected by the firer, to be fired for one press of the trigger, after which the gun stops until the trigger is released and pressed again. One of the old complaints about submachine-guns is that the muzzle tends to climb and wander off target during the firing of a burst, only the first few rounds having any effect. Using the burst-fire facility gets rid of this objection, because the effective first few rounds are the only ones fired; after that the firer starts again, and since the initial burst is so short, the gun does not wander far from the target and re-aiming is rapid.

The MP-5 was taken into use by the Federal German police and by the border guards. Other countries have evaluated it from time to time, and it has obvious attractions for any country which uses the G3 as their service rifle.

The End of the Submachine-Gun?

Enter the Assault Rifle

If Germany was the birthplace of the submachine-gun as we know it, there is every appearance that it may also turn out to be the death-bed as well. And the roots of this go back some years.

In 1943 the Germans began producing a weapon called the Maschinen Pistole 43; in fact the MP-43 was not a submachine-gun, as its name implied, but an automatic rifle, simply called a submachine-gun as a subterfuge. In the years before the war several German Army analysts had looked at the records of infantry combat during the First World War and had come up with some surprising conclusions. In the first place, infantrymen rarely fired their rifles at targets more than 400 yards away. In the second place, most infantrymen would not distinguish a target at much greater ranges than that – bearing in mind that the target was a man, crouched, in dark clothing, against a fuzzy and dark background, and not a six-foot square of white paper prominently positioned on a rifle range. Thirdly, the standard service rifles of the day were firing powerful cartridges designed to range to 2000 yards or more, a range far in excess of that which the analysis had proved was practical.

As a result a new short cartridge was developed, using much the same bullet with a truncated case and a lighter charge. This allowed accurate fire to about 600 yards, but, due to the shorter case it allowed the rifle to have a shorter action. The reduced charge meant that it developed less recoil and allowed the rifle to be lighter, and because the cartridge was smaller the infantrymen could carry more ammunition. A suitable selective-fire rifle was designed and put into production.

It was called the MP-43 in order to conceal it from Hitler, who disapproved of the theory behind the short round and the new rifle. As a machine-pistol it was therefore concealed in the monthly returns of sub-machine-gun production. Eventually, of course, the secret came out, one of Hitler's famous rages ensurd, but in the end he was persuaded to give the rifle his approval and did so by giving it a new name; he called it a *Sturmgewehr* or 'Assault Rifle'.

Since then the assault rifle has

become a standard weapon in many of the world's armies, and in these areas it has supplanted the submachine-gun.

The Soviet Army adopted the Kalashnikov AK47 in 1947 and shortly afterwards their PPSh submachine-gun disappeared from first-line service. The AK-47 is short, handy, fired full automatic or single shot, and, in short, can do anything a submachine-gun could do and also act as a rifle when required.

In the USA the Armalite rifle was adopted as an assault rifle, and since then the Colt company, who are licenced to make Arma-lites, have shortened and lightened it somewhat to produce the Colt 'Commando' submachine-gun, which looks like a rifle, fires the same .223 bullet, and, in essence, differs only in having a collapsible butt and a shorter barrel.

Similarly, the Heckler and Koch company have modified their MP-5 submachine-gun by chambering it for the .223 cartridge. This is the same round as fired by their assault rifle versions of the G3, so that the gap between the G3 and the MP-5 (known, in .223 calibre, as the HK-53) has become so small as to be practically invisible. The definition of a submachine-gun, quoted at the beginning of this book, included the requirement that it fire a pistol cartridge; but since this new breed of weapons fire rifle cartridges, they must be considered as something else. They are, indeed, nothing more than shortened assault rifles.

In spite of this move, there are still designs of submachine-gun appearing on the world markets every year. But the writing is on the wall. The US Army has removed the M3A1 from first-line and placed it in reserve stocks. An unofficial spokesman has suggested that if the British Army adopted their new 4.85-mm assault rifle, the Sterling submachine-gun will likewise go into reserve. The new French 5.56-mm assault rifle from St Etienne looks as if it will replace the MAT submachine-gun.

It has been forecast that the submachine-gun will be out of most military inventories by the mid-1980s, and if that is so it will prove to be, with the exception of the anti-tank rifle, the shortest-lived major military weapon in history.

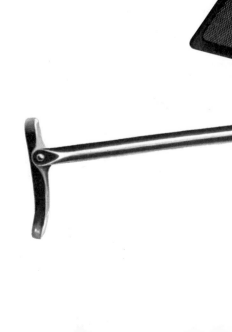

Sturmgewehr 44 7.92-mm

The first of the modern assault rifles, the StuG 44 was originally known as the MP43, though this was for political reasons rather than technical ones. Firing a short cartridge in either single shot or automatic mode, it introduced a completely new weapons philosophy, and from the moment of its arrival the submachine gun's survival as a military weapon was in question, although it was several years before the fact became apparent *Weight:* 11 lbs 4 oz *Rate of fire:* 500 rpm *Muzzle velocity:* 2125 fps

Automat Kalashnikov AK-47 7.62-mm

The AK-47 has seen wide use throughout Africa, Asia and the Middle East. Captured weapons have been incorporated into the armoury of the Israeli Army *Weight* 9 lb 8 oz *Rate of fire:* 600 rpm *Muzzle velocity:* 2330 fps

Soviet infantry in full winter equipment armed with the excellent Kalashnikov assault rifle

Colt Commando 5.56-mm

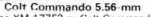

The XM 177E2 or Colt Commando is a shortened M16. During the Second Indo-Chinese War the Americans found that the M16 was too long for close quarter fighting or carrying in helicopters. The Commando is only 28 inches long with the butt telescoped. Its barrel is 10 inches long, but this reduction in length results in a considerable muzzle blast and flash which necessitates a long flash eliminator *Weight:* 6.6 lb *Rate of fire:* 700–800 rpm *Muzzle velocity:* 3000 fps

AKM

This weapon is a simplified version of the AK-47, which uses more stamped parts for ease and speed of manufacture. It has a rate reducer and a compensator, which reduces the tendency for the barrel to climb when the gun is fired on full automatic *Weight:* 6 lb 15 oz *Rate of fire:* 600 rpm *Muzzle velocity:* 2345 fps

SUBMACHINE-GUN DATA TABLE

GUN	CALIBRE	LENGTH WITH BUTT EXTENDED INS	WEIGHT EMPTY LBS	BARREL LENGTH INS	MAGAZINE TYPE AND CAPACITY	TYPE OF FIRE	RATE OF FIRE RPM
AUSTRALIA							
Austen Mk 1	9P	33.25	8.75	7.8	B 28	S	500
Owen	9P	32.0	9.35	9.85	B 33	S	700
CZECHOSLOVAKIA							
ZK 383	9P	35.4	9.4	12.8	B 30	S	700
CZ 23	9P	27.0	6.8	11.2	B 40	S	600
CZ 24	7.62	26.6	7.25	11.2	B 32	S	600
vz/61 Scorpion	7.65	20.55	2.95	4.5	B 30	S	700
DENMARK							
Madsen M1950	9P	30.71	7.6	7.87	B 32	A	550
FINLAND							
Suomi M1931	9P	34.0	11.31	12.62	D 71	S	850
FRANCE							
MAS-1938	7.65L	24.9	6.4	8.8	B 32	A	600
MAT-1949	9P	26.0	8.0	9.0	B 32	A	600
GERMANY							
Bergmann MP-18	9P	32.1	9.2	7.9	B 32	A	400
Bergmann MP-28	9P	32.0	8.8	7.8	B 32	S	500
Erma EMP	9P	37.4	9.2	11.8	B 32	S	500
Heckler & Koch MP5	9P	26.0	5.6	8.85	B 30	S	650
Heckler & Koch HK53	.223	30.1	7.4	8.85	B 40	S	650
MP-38	9P	32.8	9.0	9.9	B 32	A	500
MP-59	9P	28.8	7.0	8.3	B 30	A	620
GREAT BRITAIN							
BSA	9P	27.5	5.6	8.0	B 32	S	600
Lanchester	9P	33.75	9.6	7.9	B 50	S	600
Patchett Mk 1	9P	28.0	6.2	8.25	B 34	S	600
Sten Mk 1	9P	33.25	7.2	7.8	B 32	S	550
Sten Mk 2	9P	30.0	6.65	7.75	B 32	S	550
Sten Mk 2S (silenced)	9P	33.75	7.7	3.6	B 32	S	450
Sten Mk 3	9P	30.0	7.0	7.75	B 32	S	550

Note on abbreviations: Calibres: 9P=9-mm Parabellum; 9S=9-mm Short/.380 Auto; 9BB=9-mm Bergmann-Bayard; 9St=9-mm Steyr; 9M=9-mm Mauser Export.
Magazine type and capacity: B=box magazine; D=drum magazine
Type of fire: A=automatic only; S=selective, single shot or automatic.

GUN	CALIBRE	LENGTH WITH BUTT EXTENDED INS	WEIGHT EMPTY LBS	BARREL LENGTH INS	MAGAZINE TYPE AND CAPACITY	TYPE OF FIRE	RATE OF FIRE RPM
Sten Mk 5	9P	30.0	8.6	7.8	B 32	S	600
Sten Mk 6 (silenced)	9P	33.75	9.5	3.75	B 32	S	475
Sterling L2A4	9P	28.0	6.0	7.8	B 34	S	600
Sterling L34 (silenced)	9P	33.25	7.7	7.8	B 34	S	475

HUNGARY

GUN	CALIBRE	LENGTH WITH BUTT EXTENDED INS	WEIGHT EMPTY LBS	BARREL LENGTH INS	MAGAZINE TYPE AND CAPACITY	TYPE OF FIRE	RATE OF FIRE RPM
Danuvia M39	9M	41.25	8.2	19.65	B 40	S	750

ISRAEL

GUN	CALIBRE	LENGTH WITH BUTT EXTENDED INS	WEIGHT EMPTY LBS	BARREL LENGTH INS	MAGAZINE TYPE AND CAPACITY	TYPE OF FIRE	RATE OF FIRE RPM
Uzi	9P	25.2	7.7	10.2	B 32	S	600

ITALY

GUN	CALIBRE	LENGTH WITH BUTT EXTENDED INS	WEIGHT EMPTY LBS	BARREL LENGTH INS	MAGAZINE TYPE AND CAPACITY	TYPE OF FIRE	RATE OF FIRE RPM
Armaguerra OG44	9P	30.2	6.8	11.6	B 25	S	525
Beretta M1918	9G	33.5	7.2	12.5	B 25	A	900
Beretta M1938A	9P	37.25	9.25	12.4	B 40	S	600
Beretta M12	9P	25.4	6.6	7.9	B 40	S	550
OVP	9G	35.5	8.0	11.0	B 25	S	900
Vilar Perosa	9G	21.0	14.2	12.6	B 25×2	A	1200×2

JAPAN

GUN	CALIBRE	LENGTH WITH BUTT EXTENDED INS	WEIGHT EMPTY LBS	BARREL LENGTH INS	MAGAZINE TYPE AND CAPACITY	TYPE OF FIRE	RATE OF FIRE RPM
Type 100/1940	8mm	34.0	7.5	9.0	B 30	A	450
Type 100/1944	8mm	36.0	8.5	9.2	B 30	A	800

SOVIET UNION

GUN	CALIBRE	LENGTH WITH BUTT EXTENDED INS	WEIGHT EMPTY LBS	BARREL LENGTH INS	MAGAZINE TYPE AND CAPACITY	TYPE OF FIRE	RATE OF FIRE RPM
PPD 34	7.62	30.6	8.25	10.75	B 25	S	800
PPD-40	7.62	31.0	8.0	10.75	D 71	S	800
PPSh-41	7.62	33.1	8.0	10.6	D 71	S	900
PPS-42	7.62	35.7	6.5	10.75	B 35	A	700

SPAIN

GUN	CALIBRE	LENGTH WITH BUTT EXTENDED INS	WEIGHT EMPTY LBS	BARREL LENGTH INS	MAGAZINE TYPE AND CAPACITY	TYPE OF FIRE	RATE OF FIRE RPM
Gollat	9BB	34.5	9.75	8.5	B 36	S	600
Labora	9BB	31.75	9.4	10.25	B 36	A	750
Star Sl 35	9BB	35.4	8.2	10.6	B 30	S	300/700

SWEDEN

GUN	CALIBRE	LENGTH WITH BUTT EXTENDED INS	WEIGHT EMPTY LBS	BARREL LENGTH INS	MAGAZINE TYPE AND CAPACITY	TYPE OF FIRE	RATE OF FIRE RPM
Carl Gustav M1945	9P	31.8	7.6	8.0	B 50	S	600

SWITZERLAND

GUN	CALIBRE	LENGTH WITH BUTT EXTENDED INS	WEIGHT EMPTY LBS	BARREL LENGTH INS	MAGAZINE TYPE AND CAPACITY	TYPE OF FIRE	RATE OF FIRE RPM
MP41 SIG	9P	31.4	9.6	12.1	B 40	A	850
MP41 Furrer	9P	30.5	11.5	9.8	B 40	S	900
Rexim-Favor	9P	34.3	8.4	13.4	B 32	S	600
SIG MKMO	9M	40.25	9.8	19.25	B 40	A	900
Steyr-Solothurn	9St	33.35	8.6	7.8	B 32	S	500

UNITED STATES

GUN	CALIBRE	LENGTH WITH BUTT EXTENDED INS	WEIGHT EMPTY LBS	BARREL LENGTH INS	MAGAZINE TYPE AND CAPACITY	TYPE OF FIRE	RATE OF FIRE RPM
Atmed	.45	34.5	9.5	11.5	B 30	S	
Colt Commando	.223	31.37	6.0	9.75	B 20	S	750
Hyde-Inland M2	.45	32.1	9.25	12.10	B 20	S	525
Ingram Model 6	.45	28.5	6.5	8.0	B 20	A	600
Ingram Model 10	9P	21.57	6.75	5.75	B 32	S	900
Ingram Model 11	9S	18.0	3.25	5.12	B 32	S	1000
M3, M3A1	.45	29.8	8.15	8.0	B 30	A	400
Reising Model 50	.45	35.75	6.75	11.0	B 12	S	550
Thompson M1928	.45	33.75	10.75	10.5	B 30/D 50	S	675
Thompson M1	.45	32.0	10.5	10.5	B 20	S	700
UD M-42	9P	32.3	9.12	11.0	B 20	S	700

ARTWORK INDEX